P9-DHQ-388

CANADA

THE
NORTHEAST
pages 12–35

THE
MIDWEST
pages 62–87

ATLANTIC

OCEAN

THE WEST
pages 98–121

THE SOUTHEAST
pages 36–61

THE
SOUTHWEST
pages 88–97

BAHAMAS

CUBA

GULF OF
MEXICO

MEXICO

ATLANTIC OCEAN

120°W

100°W

80°W

60°W

60°N

40°N

60°W

20°N

80°W

NATIONAL GEOGRAPHIC KiDS

BEGINNER'S UNITED STATES ATLAS

It's YOUR country. Be a part of it!

NATIONAL GEOGRAPHIC

WASHINGTON, D.C.

Table of Contents

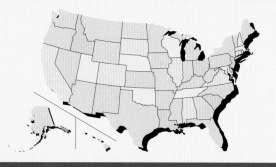

What is a Map?

An atlas is a collection of maps and pictures. A map is a drawing of a place as it looks from above. It is flat, and it is smaller than the place it shows. Learning to read a map can help you find where you are and where you want to go. **Mapping your home...**

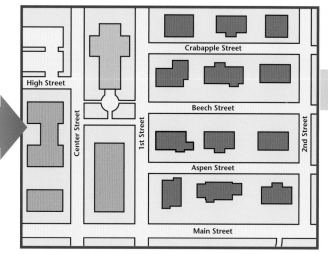

From a bird's-eye view...

if you were a bird flying directly overhead, you would see only the tops of things. You wouldn't see walls, tree trunks, tires, or feet.

On a large-scale map...

you see places from a bird's-eye view. But a map uses drawings called symbols to show things on the ground, such as houses or streets. The map of Washington, D.C., on page 10 is an example of a large-scale map.

Finding places on the map

A **map** can help you get where you want to go. A map helps you read it by showing you north, south, east and west, a key, and a scale.

▶ A **compass rose** helps you travel in the right direction. It tells you where north (N), south (S), east (E), and west (W) are on your map. Often only a north arrow is used.

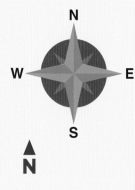

▶ A **map key** helps you understand the symbols used by the mapmaker to show things like buildings, towns, or rivers on the map.

⊛   Country capital
★   State capital
• • •   City or town
······   Boundary
    Indian Reservation
    State Park
    National Park
    National Forest
    National Grassland
    National Wildlife Refuge

0	100 miles
0	150 kilometers

◀ A **scale** tells you about distance on a map. The scale shows what length on the map represents the labeled distance on the ground.

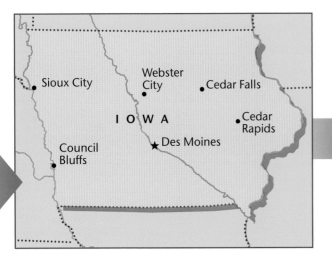

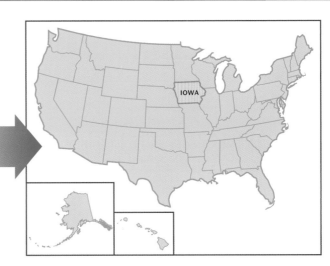

On an intermediate-scale map...

you see a place from much higher up. A town appears as a tiny dot. You can't see houses, but you can see more of the land around the town. Most maps in this atlas show a whole state with its towns and other special features.

On a small-scale map...

you can see much more of the country around the state, including other states. But on a small-scale map there is much less detail. You can no longer see most features within the state. Two states—Alaska and Hawai'i—are often shown in separate boxes or on a map of the whole continent, like on pages 6 and 7.

Map Key for the State Maps

•Aspen ....*town of under 25,000 residents*		Dry Lake
•Frankfort ....*town of 25,000 to 99,999*		Swamp
• San Jose ....*city of 100,000 to 999,999*		Glacier
• New York ....*city of 1,000,000 and over*		Sand
⊛ National capital		Lava
★ State capital		Area below sea level
▪ Point of interest		Indian Reservation, **I.R.**
+ Mountain peak with elevation above sea level		State Park, **S.P.**
• Low point with elevation below sea level		National Historic Park, **N.H.P.**

National capital

State capital

Point of interest

Mountain peak with elevation above sea level

Low point with elevation below sea level

River

Intermittent river

Canal

Interstate or selected other highway

Trail

State or national boundary

Continental divide

Lake

Intermittent lake

Dry Lake

Swamp

Glacier

Sand

Lava

Area below sea level

Indian Reservation, **I.R.**

State Park, **S.P.**

National Historic Park, **N.H.P.**
National Lakeshore
National Monument, **NAT. MON.**
National Park, **N.P.**
National Preserve, **N. PRES.**
National Recreation Area, **N.R.A.**
National River
National Scenic Area
National Seashore
National Volcanic Monument

National Forest, **N.F.**

National Grassland, **N.G.**

National Wildlife Refuge, **N.W.R.**

The Physical United States

The Land

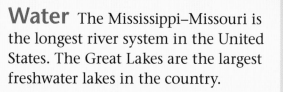

Land regions The rugged Sierra Nevadas and Rocky Mountains run north to south through the western United States. Between these mountains are dry lands with little vegetation. East of the Rockies are wide grassy plains and the older, lower Appalachian Mountains.

◀ North America is famous for its **deciduous forests**. Leaves turn fiery colors each fall!

Water The Mississippi–Missouri is the longest river system in the United States. The Great Lakes are the largest freshwater lakes in the country.

Climate The United States has many climate types—from cold Alaska to tropical Hawai'i, with milder climates in the other 48 states.

Plants The United States has forests where there is plenty of rain. Grasslands cover drier areas.

▲ Waves off the Pacific Ocean roll onto a beach along the shore of Molokai, one of the islands that make up the state of Hawai'i.

Animals There are many kinds of animals—everything from bears and deer to songbirds large and small.

Hawai'i

▼ Deserts are found in the southwestern part of the U.S. This large rock formation, called The Mitten, is in Monument Valley in Utah.

◀ The majestic bald eagle is the national bird of the United States. It is found throughout the country, but about half live in Alaska.

ARCTIC
OCEAN

GREENLAND

ASIA

Brooks Range

Yukon River

ALASKA

**Mt. McKinley
(Denali)**
*Highest elevation in
North America*

R O C K Y

Hudson
Bay

NORTH
AMERICA

PACIFIC
OCEAN

Death Valley
*Lowest elevation in
North America*

Columbia River

Sierra Nevada

Colorado River

Missouri River

G R E A T   P L A I N S

M O U N T A I N S

Mississippi River

Great Lakes

Ohio River

Appalachian Mountains

ATLANTIC
OCEAN

Rio Grande

Map Key

	Ice cap
	Tundra
	Desert
	Mountain
	Coniferous forest
	Deciduous forest
	Rain forest
	Grassland
	Wetland

Gulf of Mexico

WEST INDIES

Caribbean Sea

CENTRAL AMERICA

SOUTH
AMERICA

0   500 miles

N

0   750 kilometers

▲ Snow-capped peaks
are reflected in a clear
lake in Rocky Mountain
National Park, near
Estes Park, Colorado.

The Political United States

The People

 States The United States is made up of 50 states. Alaska and Hawai'i are separated from the rest of the country. So you can see them close up, they are shown near the bottom of the map.

 Cities Washington, D.C., is the national capital. Each state also has a capital city. New York City has the most people.

 People The United States is made up of people from almost every country in the world. Most live and work in and around cities.

 Languages English is the main language, followed by Spanish.

 Products The main products include cars, machinery, petroleum, natural gas, coal, beef, wheat, and forest products.

▶ Baseball is a popular sport in the United States along with soccer, basketball, and football.

▲ Chinese New Year is a big celebration in San Francisco. Many Chinese-Americans live there.

Seattle
Olympia ★
WASHINGTON
Portland
★ Salem
OREGON
IDAHO
★ Boise
CALIFORNIA
Sacramento ★
★ Carson City   Salt Lake City
San Francisco
San Jose
NEVADA
Las Vegas
Los Angeles ●
ARIZ
San Diego ●
Phoenix ★
Tucson

PACIFIC OCEAN

ALASKA
Juneau ★

0   400 miles
0   600 kilometers

HAWAI'I
Honolulu ★

0   150 miles
0   200 kilometers

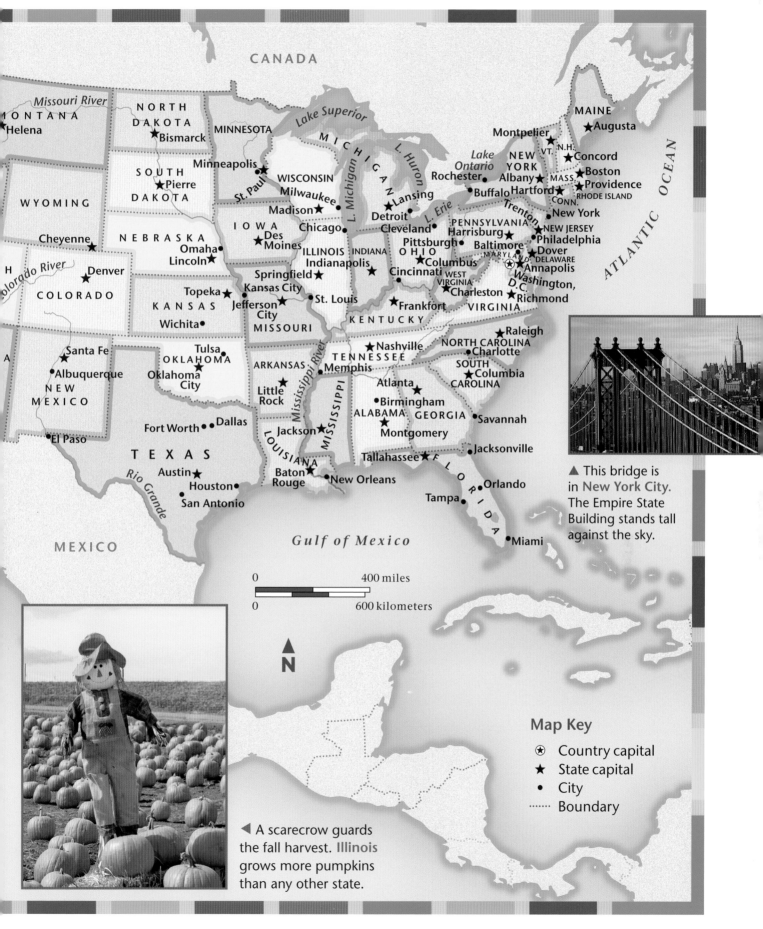

CANADA

Missouri River

MONTANA
Helena ★

NORTH
DAKOTA
Bismarck ★

MINNESOTA

Lake Superior

MICHIGAN

L. Huron

MAINE
★ Augusta

Montpelier ★

VT. N.H.
★ Concord
★ Boston
★ Providence
RHODE ISLAND

Lake
Ontario

Rochester •

NEW
YORK

Albany ★

MASS.

SOUTH
DAKOTA
★ Pierre

Minneapolis •

WISCONSIN

St. Paul ★

Milwaukee •

L. Michigan

Buffalo •

Hartford ★

CONN.

New York ★

WYOMING

Madison ★

IOWA

Des
Moines ★

Chicago •

★ Lansing

Detroit •

Cleveland •

L. Erie

Trenton

PENNSYLVANIA

Harrisburg ★

Pittsburgh •

NEW JERSEY

★ Philadelphia

Cheyenne ★

NEBRASKA

Omaha •

Lincoln ★

ILLINOIS

INDIANA

OHIO

Columbus ★

Baltimore •

Dover ★

DELAWARE

Colorado River

Denver •

COLORADO

Indianapolis ★

Springfield ★

Cincinnati •

WEST
VIRGINIA

MARYLAND

⊛ Annapolis

Washington,
D.C.

Topeka ★

Kansas City •

St. Louis •

Charleston ★

Richmond ★

KANSAS

Jefferson
City ★

Frankfort ★

VIRGINIA

ATLANTIC OCEAN

Wichita •

MISSOURI

KENTUCKY

Santa Fe ★

Tulsa •

OKLAHOMA

ARKANSAS

Mississippi River

Nashville ★

TENNESSEE

Raleigh ★

NORTH CAROLINA

Charlotte •

Albuquerque •

NEW
MEXICO

Oklahoma
City ★

Memphis •

SOUTH
★ Columbia
CAROLINA

Little
Rock ★

Atlanta ★

El Paso •

Fort Worth • Dallas •

Jackson ★

MISSISSIPPI

Birmingham •

ALABAMA

GEORGIA

Savannah •

LOUISIANA

TEXAS

Austin ★

Baton
Rouge ★

Houston •

New Orleans •

San Antonio •

Montgomery ★

Tallahassee ★

FLORIDA

Jacksonville •

MEXICO

Gulf of Mexico

Orlando •

Tampa •

Rio Grande

0   400 miles

0   600 kilometers

Miami •

N

▲ This bridge is
in New York City.
The Empire State
Building stands tall
against the sky.

Map Key

⊛ Country capital

★ State capital

• City

...... Boundary

◄ A scarecrow guards
the fall harvest. Illinois
grows more pumpkins
than any other state.

The District of Columbia

The National Capital Washington, D.C.

Land & Water The National Mall, the Potomac River, and the Anacostia River are important land and water features of the District of Columbia.

Statehood The District of Columbia was founded in 1790, but it is not a state.

People & Places The District of Columbia's population is 591,833. Known as Washington, D.C., the city is the seat of the U.S. government.

Fun Fact The flag of the District of Columbia, with three red stars and two red stripes, is based on the shield in George Washington's family coat of arms.

▶ The **Smithsonian Institution**, the world's largest museum, is actually made up of 19 museums. It was established in 1846 and is sometimes referred to as the nation's attic because of its large collections.

◀ **Abraham Lincoln**, who was President during the Civil War and a strong opponent of slavery, is remembered in a memorial that houses this seated statue at the west end of the National Mall.

Washington, D.C., Flag

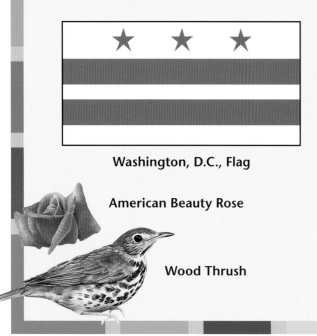

American Beauty Rose

Wood Thrush

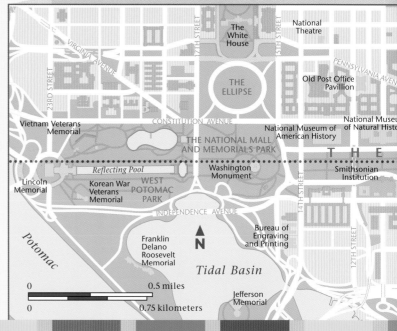

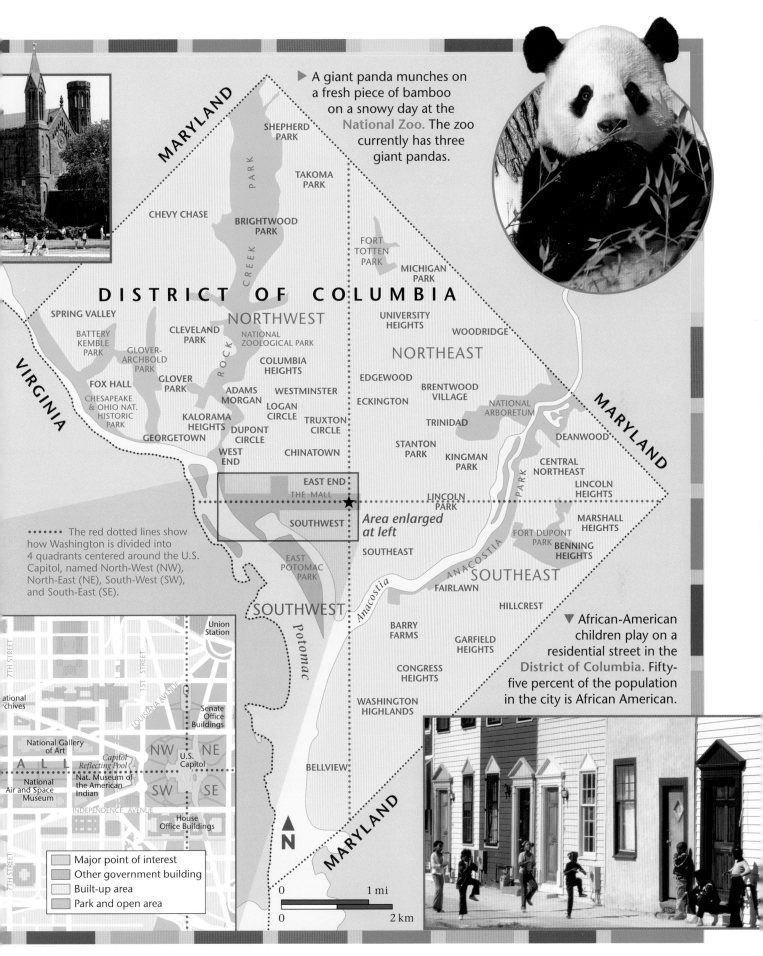

▶ A giant panda munches on a fresh piece of bamboo on a snowy day at the **National Zoo.** The zoo currently has three giant pandas.

MARYLAND

SHEPHERD PARK

TAKOMA PARK

CHEVY CHASE

BRIGHTWOOD PARK

PARK

CREEK

FORT TOTTEN PARK

MICHIGAN PARK

DISTRICT OF COLUMBIA

SPRING VALLEY

NORTHWEST

UNIVERSITY HEIGHTS

WOODRIDGE

BATTERY KEMBLE PARK

CLEVELAND PARK

NATIONAL ZOOLOGICAL PARK

NORTHEAST

VIRGINIA

GLOVER-ARCHBOLD PARK

ROCK

COLUMBIA HEIGHTS

EDGEWOOD

BRENTWOOD VILLAGE

FOX HALL

GLOVER PARK

ADAMS MORGAN

WESTMINSTER

ECKINGTON

NATIONAL ARBORETUM

CHESAPEAKE & OHIO NAT. HISTORIC PARK

KALORAMA HEIGHTS

LOGAN CIRCLE

TRINIDAD

GEORGETOWN

DUPONT CIRCLE

TRUXTON CIRCLE

STANTON PARK

DEANWOOD

WEST END

CHINATOWN

KINGMAN PARK

CENTRAL NORTHEAST

MARYLAND

EAST END

THE MALL

LINCOLN PARK

LINCOLN HEIGHTS

★

Area enlarged at left

SOUTHWEST

PARK

MARSHALL HEIGHTS

•••••• The red dotted lines show how Washington is divided into 4 quadrants centered around the U.S. Capitol, named North-West (NW), North-East (NE), South-West (SW), and South-East (SE).

SOUTHEAST

FORT DUPONT PARK

BENNING HEIGHTS

EAST POTOMAC PARK

ANACOSTIA

SOUTHEAST

FAIRLAWN

Anacostia

HILLCREST

SOUTHWEST

▼ African-American children play on a residential street in the **District of Columbia.** Fifty-five percent of the population in the city is African American.

Potomac

BARRY FARMS

GARFIELD HEIGHTS

Union Station

CONGRESS HEIGHTS

7TH STREET

1ST STREET

LOUISIANA AVENUE

Senate Office Buildings

WASHINGTON HIGHLANDS

National Archives

National Gallery of Art

Capitol Reflecting Pool

NW

NE

U.S. Capitol

ALL

National Air and Space Museum

Nat. Museum of the American Indian

SW

SE

BELLVIEW

INDEPENDENCE AVENUE

House Office Buildings

N

MARYLAND

0   1 mi

0   2 km

Major point of interest

Other government building

Built-up area

Park and open area

The Northeast

Early settlers and traders from Europe established colonies in the Northeast region. These colonies eventually became states. Over time, people came from countries all around the world to live in the United States. Many of these people arrived through large port cities in the Northeast, including New York City, Boston, and Baltimore. They brought with them different customs, languages, and beliefs that make the Northeast a region of great variety. Today the Northeast region includes the country's financial center, New York City, and its political capital, Washington, D.C.

Water plunges as much as 110 feet (34 m) over the American Falls on the Niagara River near New York's border with Canada, our neighbor to the north. Black bears are common in the forests of the region.

Connecticut

 Land & Water Mount Frissell, the Connecticut River, and Long Island Sound are important land and water features of Connecticut.

Statehood Connecticut became the 5th state in 1788.

People & Places Connecticut's population is 3,501,252. Hartford is the state capital. The largest city is Bridgeport.

Fun Fact The sperm whale, Connecticut's state animal, is known for its massive head. Its brain is larger than that of any other creature known to have lived on Earth.

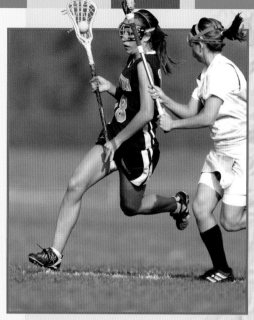

▲ Girls' lacrosse is popular in schools and colleges in Connecticut and across the U.S. It was adapted from a Native American game.

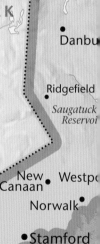

Mt. Fris
2,380 ft
725 m
Lake

MACEDONI
BROOK
STATE PARK

New
Milford

Lake
Candlewood

NEW YORK

Danbu

Ridgefield

Saugatuck
Reservoi

New
Canaan • Westpo

Norwalk

• Stamford
• Greenwich

Connecticut State Flag

**Mountain Laurel
State Flower**

**Robin
State Bird**

◄ The *Charles W. Morgan*, launched in 1841, but now docked in Mystic Seaport, is the last surviving wooden whaling ship in the U.S.

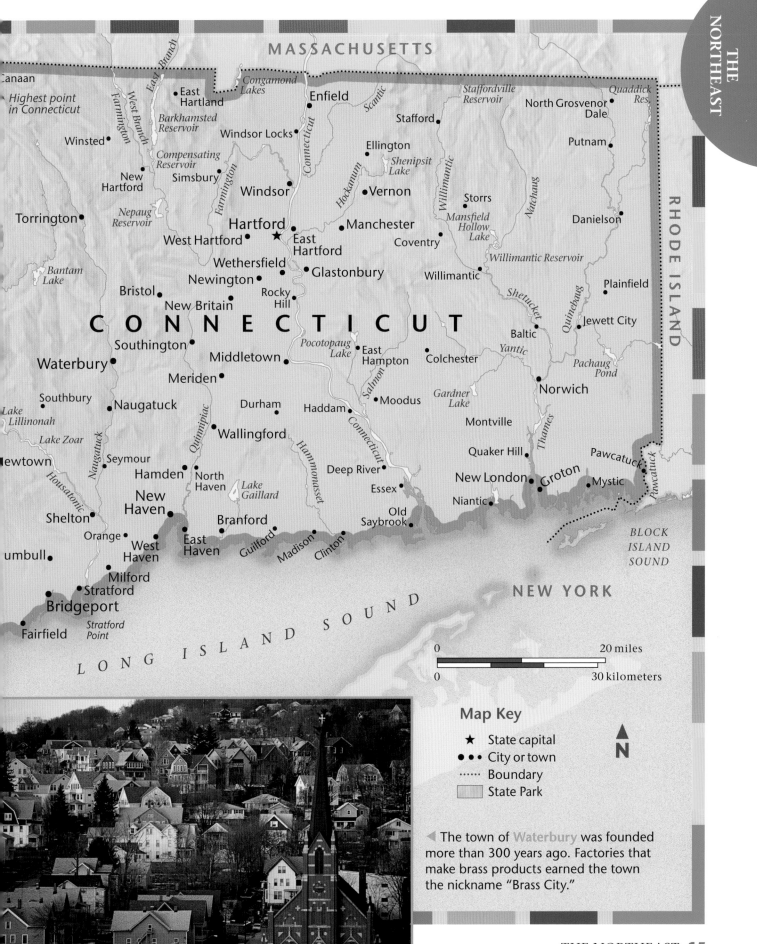

MASSACHUSETTS

RHODE ISLAND

Canaan

Highest point in Connecticut

East Hartland

Congamond Lakes

Enfield

Staffordville Reservoir

Quaddick Res.

North Grosvenor Dale

Barkhamsted Reservoir

Windsor Locks

Stafford

Putnam

Winsted

Compensating Reservoir

Ellington

Shenipsit Lake

New Hartford

Simsbury

Windsor

Vernon

Storrs

Danielson

Torrington

Nepaug Reservoir

Hartford

Manchester

Mansfield Hollow Lake

West Hartford

East Hartford

Coventry

Willimantic Reservoir

Bantam Lake

Wethersfield

Glastonbury

Willimantic

Plainfield

Bristol

Newington

Rocky Hill

New Britain

C O N N E C T I C U T

Baltic

Jewett City

Southington

Pocotopaug Lake

East Hampton

Colchester

Norwich

Waterbury

Middletown

Meriden

Gardner Lake

Pachaug Pond

Southbury

Naugatuck

Durham

Haddam

Moodus

Lake Lillinonah

Wallingford

Montville

Lake Zoar

Seymour

Deep River

Quaker Hill

Pawcatuck

ewtown

Hamden

North Haven

Lake Gaillard

Essex

New London

Groton

Mystic

New Haven

Branford

Old Saybrook

Niantic

Shelton

Orange

East Haven

Guilford

Madison

Clinton

BLOCK ISLAND SOUND

umbull

West Haven

Milford

Stratford

NEW YORK

Bridgeport

Fairfield

Stratford Point

L O N G   I S L A N D   S O U N D

0   20 miles

0   30 kilometers

Map Key

★ State capital

••• City or town

...... Boundary

▨ State Park

N

◀ The town of Waterbury was founded more than 300 years ago. Factories that make brass products earned the town the nickname "Brass City."

Delaware

Land & Water Barrier Islands, Cypress Swamp, and Delaware Bay are important land and water features of Delaware.

Statehood Delaware became the 1st state in 1787.

People & Places Delaware's population is 873,092. Dover is the state capital. The largest city is Wilmington.

Fun Fact Each year contestants bring pumpkins and launching machines to the Punkin Chunkin World Championship in Bridgeville to see who can toss their big orange squash the farthest.

▲ The Delmarva Peninsula, with nearly 2,000 poultry growers, is a major producing area for chickens. The industry's trade association is located in **Georgetown**.

▶ Patriotic boys wave American flags at a Delaware Motorsports track near **Delmar**. Racing fans have come to the tracks since they opened in 1963.

▼ Bright-colored umbrellas dot **Bethany Beach**. Sun, sand, and surf attract thousands of vacationers each year to Delaware's shore.

Delaware State Flag

DECEMBER 7, 1787

Peach Blossom State Flower

Blue Hen Chicken State Bird

448 ft
137 m ← *Highest point in Delaware*

PENNSYLVANIA

Claymont
Hockessin
Wilmington
Elsmere
Newport
Newark
New Castle
Bear
Delaware City
Glasgow
Chesapeake and Delaware Canal
Port Penn
Middletown
Odessa

Brandywine Cr.
Christina
Delaware

NEW JERSEY

Pea Patch Island
Reedy Island

Map Key

★ State capital
●●● City or town
•••• Boundary
▨ National Wildlife Refuge

Liston Pt.
Noxontown Pond
Townsend
Smyrna
Smyrna
Clayton
BOMBAY HOOK
Leipsic
NATIONAL
Cheswold
WILDLIFE
REFUGE
Deepwater Point

Bombay Hook Island

| 0 | 10 miles |
| 0 | 15 kilometers |

St. Jones
★ Dover
Camden
Marydel
Kitts Hummock
Bowers Beach

DELAWARE

MARYLAND

Choptank

Felton
Frederica

Harrington
Houston
Milford
Slaughter Beach
Lincoln
PRIME HOOK
NATIONAL
Broadkill Beach
WILDLIFE
REFUGE

Delaware Bay

N

The Harbor of Refuge Light sits near the mouth of Delaware Bay, where it marks a safe channel for ships. The current light was erected in 1926.

Greenwood
Ellendale
Milton
Nassau
HARBOR OF REFUGE LIGHTHOUSE
Cape Henlopen

Bridgeville
Lewes & Rehoboth Canal
Harbeson
Lewes
Georgetown
Midway
Rehoboth Beach
Dewey Beach

ATLANTIC

Rehoboth Bay

OCEAN

Marshyhope Creek
PENINSULA

Seaford
Nanticoke

Oak Orchard
Indian River Bay
Indian River Inlet
Millsboro

Barrier Islands

Laurel
Dagsboro
Ocean View
Bethany Beach
Assawoman Canal
Frankford

Cypress Swamp
Delmar
Selbyville
Fenwick Island

The Northeast

Maine

Land & Water The Appalachian Mountains, Mt. Katahdin, and the Gulf of Maine are important land and water features of Maine.

Statehood Maine became the 23rd state in 1820.

People & Places Maine's population is 1,316,456. Augusta is the state capital. The largest city is Portland.

Fun Fact During the last ice age, glaciers carved hundreds of bays and inlets along Maine's shoreline and created some 2,000 islands off the coast.

▲ More than 60 lighthouses line Maine's rocky coastline, warning ships of danger. The oldest lighthouse, Portland Head Light, is located at Cape Elizabeth.

◄ Each year Rockland hosts the Maine Lobster Festival. This celebration of the state's popular seafood delicacy attracts visitors from far and near.

▼ Moose are North America's largest deer, averaging 6 feet (2 m) tall at the shoulders. This female stands knee-deep in grass near Rangeley Lake.

Maine State Flag

White Pine Cone and Tassel State Flower

Chickadee State Bird

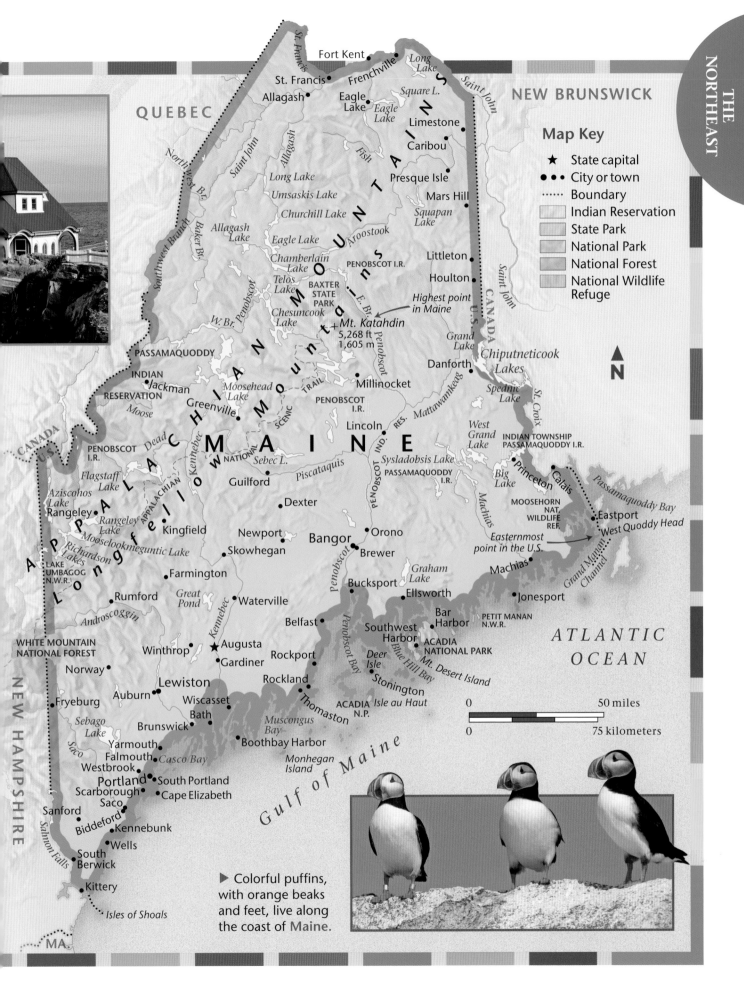

QUEBEC

NEW BRUNSWICK

Map Key

★ State capital
• • • City or town
• • • • Boundary
Indian Reservation
State Park
National Park
National Forest
National Wildlife Refuge

Fort Kent
St. Francis
Frenchville
Long Lake
Allagash
Eagle Lake
Square L.
Eagle Lake
Limestone
Caribou
Presque Isle
Mars Hill
Squapan Lake
Littleton
Houlton

Saint John
Northwest Br.
Saint John
Allagash
Fish

Long Lake
Umsaskis Lake
Churchill Lake
Aroostook

Allagash Lake
Eagle Lake
Chamberlain Lake
Telos Lake
Chesuncook Lake

PENOBSCOT I.R.

BAXTER STATE PARK

Highest point in Maine

Mt. Katahdin
5,268 ft
1,605 m

Grand Lake
Chiputneticook Lakes

Danforth

Spednic Lake
St. Croix

CANADA
U.S.

Saint John

PASSAMAQUODDY
INDIAN RESERVATION

Jackman

Moose

PENOBSCOT I.R.

Moosehead Lake

Greenville

Millinocket

PENOBSCOT I.R.

West Grand Lake

INDIAN TOWNSHIP PASSAMAQUODDY I.R.

CANADA
U.S.

Flagstaff Lake

Dead

Kennebec

NATIONAL

Sebec L.

Lincoln

PENOBSCOT IND. RES.

Mattawamkeag

Sysladobsis Lake

PASSAMAQUODDY I.R.

Big Lake

Princeton
Calais

Passamaquoddy Bay

MOOSEHORN NAT. WILDLIFE REF.

Eastport
West Quoddy Head

Easternmost point in the U.S.

APPALACHIAN MOUNTAINS

MAINE

Guilford

Piscataquis

Machias

Grand Manan Channel

Aziscohos Lake
Rangeley
Rangeley Lake
Mooselookmeguntic Lake
Richardson Lakes

LAKE UMBAGOG N.W.R.

Kingfield

Dexter

Newport
Skowhegan

Bangor
Brewer

Orono

Graham Lake

Machias

Jonesport

Farmington

Great Pond

Waterville

Kennebec

Bucksport

Ellsworth

Bar Harbor

PETIT MANAN N.W.R.

ATLANTIC OCEAN

Rumford

Androscoggin

Belfast

Penobscot Bay

Southwest Harbor

ACADIA NATIONAL PARK

Mt. Desert Island

WHITE MOUNTAIN NATIONAL FOREST

Winthrop
★ Augusta
Gardiner

Rockport

Deer Isle

Blue Hill Bay

Norway

Rockland

Stonington

Lewiston

Auburn

Wiscasset
Bath

Thomaston

ACADIA N.P.

Isle au Haut

Fryeburg

Sebago Lake

Brunswick

Muscongus Bay

Saco

Yarmouth
Falmouth
Westbrook

Casco Bay

Boothbay Harbor

Monhegan Island

Gulf of Maine

Portland
South Portland
Scarborough
Saco
Cape Elizabeth

Sanford

Biddeford
Kennebunk

Salmon Falls

Wells

South Berwick

Kittery

Isles of Shoals

NEW HAMPSHIRE

MA.

N

0   50 miles
0   75 kilometers

▶ Colorful puffins, with orange beaks and feet, live along the coast of Maine.

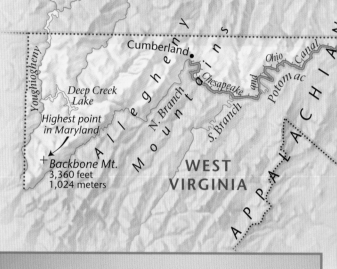

Maryland

Land & Water The Appalachian Mountains, Potomac River, and Chesapeake Bay are important land and water features of Maryland.

Statehood Maryland became the 7th state in 1788.

People & Places Maryland's population is 5,633,597. Annapolis is the state's capital. The largest city is Baltimore.

Fun Fact The name of Baltimore's professional football team—the Ravens—may have been inspired by a poem written by the famous American author Edgar Allan Poe, who lived in Baltimore in the mid-1800s.

▲ Sailing is a popular pastime on Maryland's **Chesapeake Bay**. In the background, the Bay Bridge stretches 4.3 miles (6.9 km) across the waters of the Bay.

Maryland State Flag

Black-eyed Susan State Flower

Northern (Baltimore) Oriole State Bird

▲ Since the early 1700s, **Baltimore**, near the upper Chesapeake Bay, has been a major seaport and focus of trade, industry, and immigration.

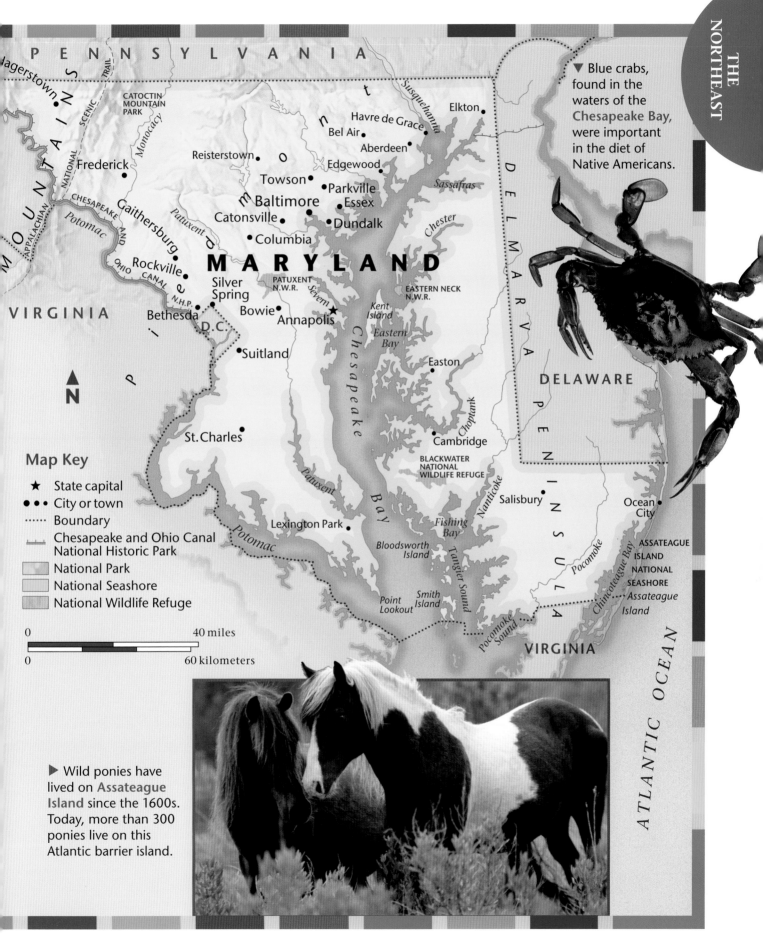

P E N N S Y L V A N I A

Hagerstown

CATOCTIN
MOUNTAIN
PARK

Elkton

Havre de Grace

Bel Air

Aberdeen

Frederick

Reisterstown

Edgewood

Monocacy

Susquehanna

Sassafras

Towson

Parkville

Essex

M A R Y L A N D

Baltimore

Catonsville

Dundalk

Chester

Columbia

Gaithersburg

Patuxent

DELMARVA

Rockville

CHESAPEAKE AND OHIO CANAL

Potomac

APPALACHIAN

N.H.P.

Silver
Spring

PATUXENT
N.W.R.

Severn

EASTERN NECK
N.W.R.

Kent
Island

Bethesda

Bowie

Annapolis ★

*Eastern
Bay*

VIRGINIA

D.C.

Suitland

Chesapeake

Easton

DELAWARE

P I E

St. Charles

Choptank

Cambridge

BLACKWATER
NATIONAL
WILDLIFE REFUGE

P E N I N S U L A

Patuxent

Bay

Nanticoke

Salisbury

Ocean
City

Map Key

★ State capital

●●● City or town

⋯⋯ Boundary

Chesapeake and Ohio Canal
National Historic Park

National Park

National Seashore

National Wildlife Refuge

Lexington Park

Potomac

*Bloodsworth
Island*

*Fishing
Bay*

Tangier Sound

Pocomoke

ASSATEAGUE
ISLAND
NATIONAL
SEASHORE

*Assateague
Island*

Chincoteague Bay

0   40 miles

0   60 kilometers

*Point
Lookout*

*Smith
Island*

VIRGINIA

*Pocomoke
Sound*

A T L A N T I C   O C E A N

N

▼ Blue crabs,
found in the
waters of the
Chesapeake Bay,
were important
in the diet of
Native Americans.

▶ Wild ponies have
lived on **Assateague
Island** since the 1600s.
Today, more than 300
ponies live on this
Atlantic barrier island.

Massachusetts

 Land & Water The Berkshire Mountains, Cape Cod, and Nantucket Sound are important land and water features of Massachusetts.

 Statehood Massachusetts became the 6th state in 1788.

 People & Places Massachusetts's population is 6,497,967. Boston is the state capital and the largest city.

Fun Fact In 1891, James Naismith invented the game of basketball as a form of physical activity. Today, the Basketball Hall of Fame is located in Springfield in his honor.

▲ Fenway Park in **Boston** is home to the Red Sox major league baseball team. The park was named for a Boston neighborhood known as the Fens.

▼ Cranberries, grown in fields called bogs, are Massachusetts's largest agricultural crop, employing more than 5,000 people. An annual cranberry harvest festival is held in **Wareham**.

Massachusetts State Flag

Chickadee State Bird

Mayflower State Flower

Map labels:
VERMONT
NEW YORK
North Adams
Mt. Greylock 3,491 ft 1,064 m — Highest point in Massachuset
Deerfield
Greenfield
Hoosic
Hoosic Range
TRAIL
SCENIC
NATIONAL
APPALACHIAN
The Berkshires
Middle Branch
West Branch
Westfield
W. Branch Farmington
Pittsfield
Stockbridge
Housatonic
Taconic Range
PIONEE
MAS
Northampton
Easthampton
Amher
Connecticut
VALLEY
Holyoke
Ludlow
Chicopee
Chicope
Otis Res.
Westfield
Springfield
Agawam
CONNECTICUT

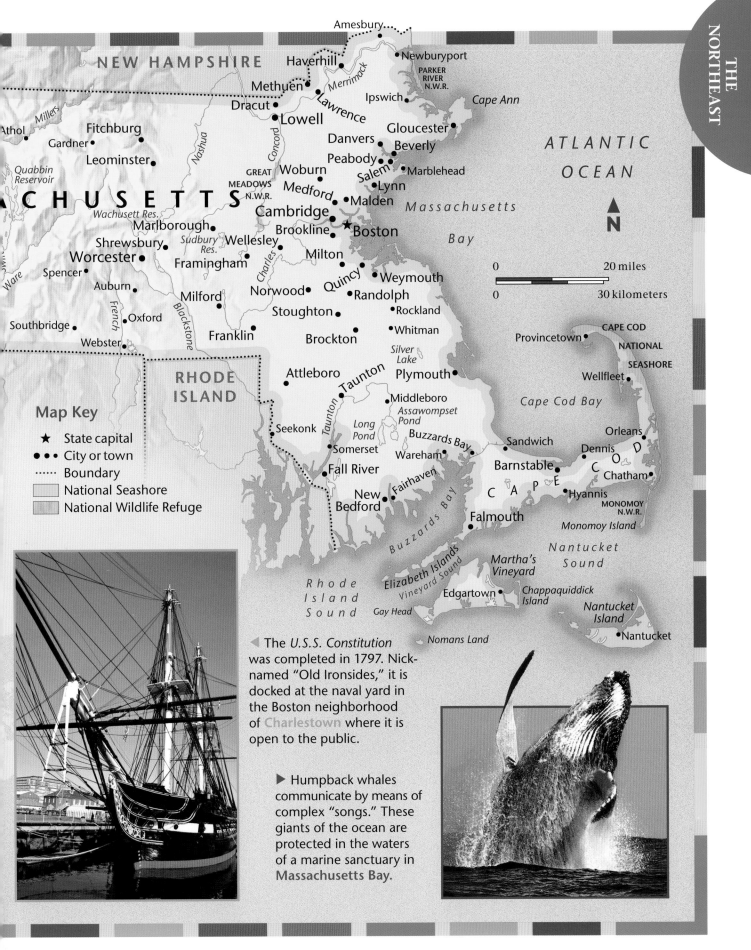

NEW HAMPSHIRE

Amesbury

Haverhill

Newburyport

Methuen

PARKER RIVER N.W.R.

Dracut

Lawrence

Ipswich

Cape Ann

Lowell

Merrimack

Athol

Fitchburg

Danvers

Gloucester

Gardner

Beverly

Leominster

Peabody

Marblehead

Nashua

Salem

Quabbin Reservoir

GREAT MEADOWS N.W.R.

Woburn

Lynn

ATLANTIC OCEAN

ＣＨＵＳＥＴＴＳ

Wachusett Res.

Medford

Malden

Massachusetts Bay

Concord

Cambridge

N

Marlborough

Brookline

★ Boston

Shrewsbury

Sudbury Res.

Wellesley

Milton

0   20 miles

Worcester

Framingham

0   30 kilometers

Spencer

Charles

Quincy

Weymouth

Auburn

Norwood

Randolph

Rockland

Milford

Stoughton

Whitman

French

Oxford

Blackstone

Provincetown

CAPE COD NATIONAL SEASHORE

Southbridge

Franklin

Brockton

Silver Lake

Plymouth

Wellfleet

Webster

Attleboro

Taunton

Cape Cod Bay

RHODE ISLAND

Taunton

Middleboro

Orleans

Assawompset Pond

Sandwich

Dennis

Map Key

Seekonk

Long Pond

Buzzards Bay

Barnstable

Chatham

★ State capital

Somerset

Wareham

Hyannis

••• City or town

Fall River

Buzzards Bay

MONOMOY N.W.R.

····· Boundary

Fairhaven

C A P E   C O D

National Seashore

New Bedford

Falmouth

Monomoy Island

National Wildlife Refuge

Buzzards Bay

Nantucket Sound

Rhode Island Sound

Elizabeth Islands

Martha's Vineyard

Vineyard Sound

Edgartown

Chappaquiddick Island

Nantucket Island

Gay Head

Nomans Land

Nantucket

◀ The *U.S.S. Constitution* was completed in 1797. Nicknamed "Old Ironsides," it is docked at the naval yard in the Boston neighborhood of Charlestown where it is open to the public.

▶ Humpback whales communicate by means of complex "songs." These giants of the ocean are protected in the waters of a marine sanctuary in Massachusetts Bay.

The Northeast

New Hampshire

 Land & Water The White Mountains, Mount Washington, and the Merrimack River are important land and water features of New Hampshire.

Statehood New Hampshire became the 9th state in 1788.

People & Places New Hampshire's population is 1,315,809. Concord is the state capital. The largest city is Manchester.

Fun Fact The first potato grown in the United States was planted in 1719 in Londonderry on the Common Field, now known simply as the Commons.

▲ A golden dome topped by a war eagle rises above New Hampshire's State House in **Concord**. The pale granite building was completed in 1819.

◄ Bitter cold and heavy snow are common in the **White Mountains** of New Hampshire, where snow tubing and skiing are popular winter sports.

New Hampshire State Flag

▼ **Mount Washington** rises above trees rich with autumn colors. But soon winter will arrive, bringing some of the most extreme weather in the world.

Purple Lilac
State Flower

Purple Finch
State Bird

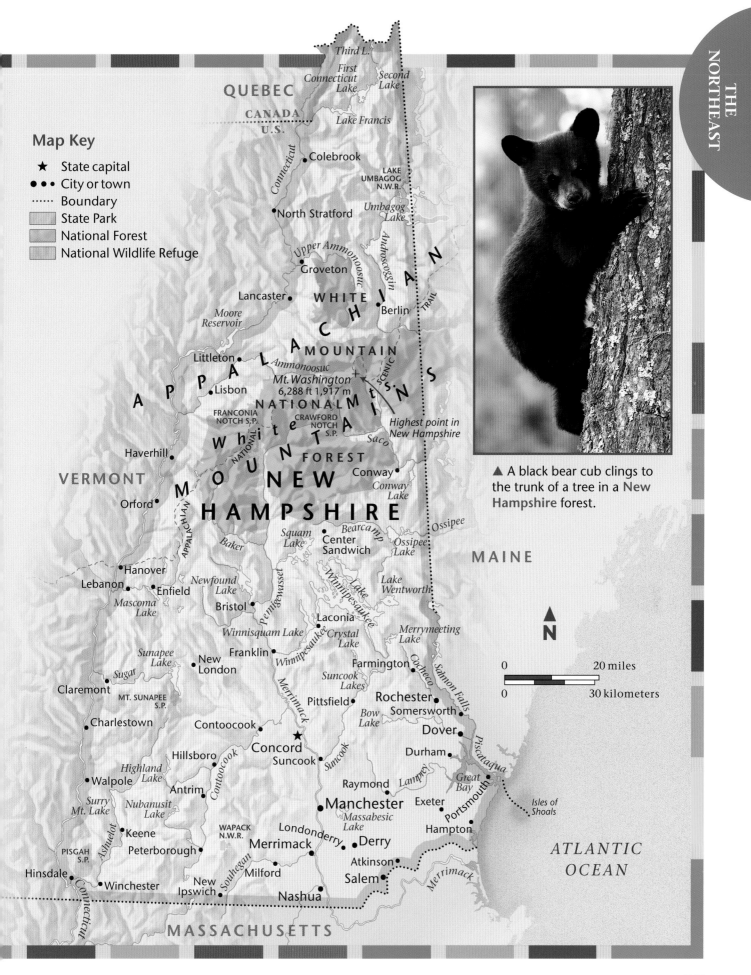

Map Key

★ State capital
●●● City or town
······ Boundary
State Park
National Forest
National Wildlife Refuge

QUEBEC

CANADA
U.S.

Third L.

First
Connecticut
Lake

Second
Lake

Lake Francis

● Colebrook

LAKE
UMBAGOG
N.W.R.

● North Stratford

Umbagog
Lake

Connecticut

Upper Ammonoosuc

● Groveton

Lancaster ●

WHITE

● Berlin

Androscoggin

APPALACHIAN

Moore
Reservoir

A P P A L

Littleton ●

● Lisbon

A MOUNTAIN

Ammonoosuc

FRANCONIA
NOTCH S.P.

+ Mt. Washington
6,288 ft 1,917 m

NATIONAL

SCENIC

CRAWFORD
NOTCH
S.P.

M T N S.

MOUNTAINS

Highest point in
New Hampshire

Haverhill ●

White

NATIONAL

Saco

A

FOREST

VERMONT

M

Conway ●

MOUNTAINS

NEW

Conway
Lake

Orford ●

HAMPSHIRE

● Hanover

APPALACHIAN

Squam
Lake

Bearcamp

Center
Sandwich

Baker

MAINE

Ossipee
Lake

Ossipee

▲ A black bear cub clings to
the trunk of a tree in a **New
Hampshire** forest.

Lebanon ●
Enfield ●

Newfound
Lake

Pemigewasset

Winnipesaukee

Lake

Lake
Wentworth

Mascoma
Lake

Bristol ●

N

Winnisquam Lake

Laconia ●

Winnipesaukee

Crystal
Lake

Merrymeeting
Lake

0   20 miles

Sunapee
Lake

Franklin ●

New
London ●

Merrimack

Farmington ●

Cocheco

Salmon Falls

0   30 kilometers

Sugar

Claremont ●

MT. SUNAPEE
S.P.

Suncook
Lakes

Pittsfield ●

Rochester ●
Somersworth ●

Charlestown ●

Contoocook ●

Bow
Lake

Dover ●

Hillsboro ●

★ Concord
Suncook ●

Suncook

Durham ●

Piscataqua

Highland
Lake

Antrim ●

Contoocook

Raymond ●

Lamprey

Great
Bay

Walpole ●

Manchester ●

Exeter ●

Portsmouth ●

Isles of
Shoals

Surry
Mt. Lake

Nubanusit
Lake

WAPACK
N.W.R.

Massabesic
Lake

Londonderry ●

Hampton ●

Keene ●

Peterborough ●

Merrimack

● Derry

ATLANTIC
OCEAN

PISGAH
S.P.

Milford ●

Atkinson ●

Hinsdale ●

Winchester ●

New
Ipswich ●

Southegan

Salem ●

Merrimack

Ashuelot

Connecticut

Nashua ●

MASSACHUSETTS

New Jersey

Land & Water The Kittatinny Mountains, Cape May, and the Delaware River are important land and water features in New Jersey.

Statehood New Jersey became the 3rd state in 1787.

People & Places New Jersey's population is 8,682,661. Trenton is the state capital. The largest city is Newark.

Fun Fact The first dinosaur skeleton found in North America was excavated at Haddonfield in 1858. It was named Hadrosaurus in honor of its discovery site.

▲ Sandy beaches on the Atlantic coast of New Jersey attract vacationers from near and far. Roller coasters are just one of the exciting rides in amusement parks along the shore.

◀ Street names, such as Boardwalk and Park Place, in the popular board game of Monopoly are taken from actual street names in Atlantic City.

New Jersey State Flag

America Goldfinch State Bird

Violet State Flower

▼ The skylines of Jersey City (left) and New York City (in the distance at right) glow in the evening light. Jersey City, second largest city in the state, is home to many large corporations.

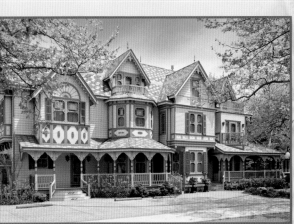

▲ Victorian-style houses line a street in **Cape May**. The town is a national historic landmark and the country's oldest seashore resort.

▲ New Jersey, known as the **Garden State**, is a leading producer of fresh fruits and vegetables.

Map Key

★ State capital
●●● City or town
····· Boundary
National Historic Park
National Recreation Area
National Wildlife Refuge

High Point 1,803 ft 550 m
Highest point in New Jersey

NEW YORK

Highland Lakes
Ringwood
Newton
Sparta
Wanaque Reservoir
Ramsey
Wanaque
Ridgewood
Paramus
Hopatcong
Lake Hopatcong
Wayne
Paterson
Clifton
Passaic
Hackensack
Dover
Morristown
MORRISTOWN N.H.P.
Hackettstown
GREAT SWAMP N.W.R.
Newark
Jersey City
Phillipsburg
Bernardsville
Berkeley Heights
Elizabeth
Bayonne
Ellis Island
High Bridge
Round Valley Res.
Somerville
Raritan
Lower Bay
Flemington
Somerville
Edison
Sandy Hook
Sandy Hook Bay
GATEWAY N.R.A.
New Brunswick
East Brunswick
Princeton
Mercerville
Red Bank
Eatontown
Long Branch
Trenton
White Horse
Freehold
Neptune
Asbury Park

NEW JERSEY

PENNSYLVANIA

Burlington
Willingboro
Mount Holly
Lakewood
Point Pleasant
Camden
Pennsauken
Cherry Hill
Toms River
Seaside Heights
Woodbury
Lindenwold
Barnegat Bay
Glassboro
Long Beach Island
Pennsville
Hammonton
Ship Bottom
SUPAWNA MEADOWS N.W.R.
E. B. FORSYTHE N.W.R.
Little Egg Harbor
Beach Haven
Vineland
Great Bay
Bridgeton
Millville
Pleasantville
Brigantine
Somers Point
Atlantic City
Ventnor City
Ocean City
Woodbine
ATLANTIC OCEAN

DELAWARE
Delaware Bay
Villas
Cape May Court House
CAPE MAY
Wildwood
Cape May

0   20 miles
0   30 kilometers

THE NORTHEAST **27**

New York

Land & Water The Adirondack Mountains, the Finger Lakes, and the Hudson River are important land and water features of New York.

Statehood New York became the 11th state in 1788.

People & Places New York's population is 19,490,297. Albany is the state capital. The largest city is New York City.

Fun Fact The Erie Canal, built in the 1820s between Albany and Buffalo, allowed ships to travel from the Atlantic Ocean to the Great Lakes. The canal helped New York City become a major trading center.

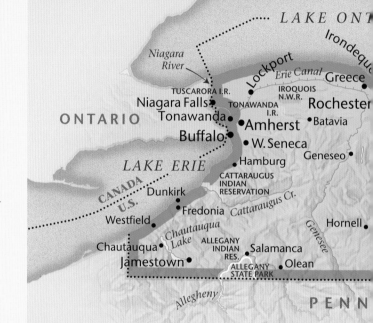

New York State Flag

Eastern Bluebird State Bird

Rose State Flower

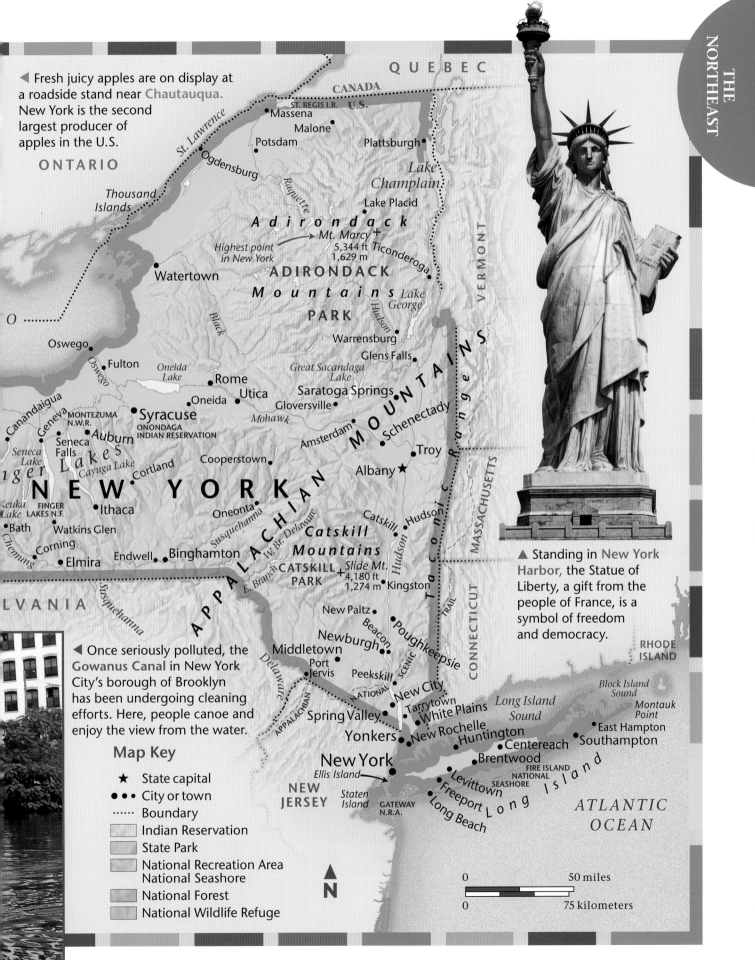

◀ Fresh juicy apples are on display at a roadside stand near Chautauqua. New York is the second largest producer of apples in the U.S.

QUEBEC

CANADA
U.S.

ONTARIO

St. Lawrence

Ogdensburg

Thousand
Islands

ST. REGIS I.R.

Massena

Malone

Potsdam

Plattsburgh

Lake
Champlain

Raquette

Lake Placid

A d i r o n d a c k

→ Mt. Marcy +
Highest point
in New York
5,344 ft
1,629 m

Ticonderoga

Watertown

ADIRONDACK

M o u n t a i n s

PARK

Lake
George

Black

Hudson

Oswego

Warrensburg

Oswego

Fulton

Oneida
Lake

Glens Falls

Great Sacandaga
Lake

Rome

Utica

Saratoga Springs

Canandaigua

Oneida

Gloversville

V E R M O N T

Geneva

MONTEZUMA
N.W.R.

Syracuse

Mohawk

Amsterdam

Schenectady

Auburn

ONONDAGA
INDIAN RESERVATION

Seneca
Lake

Seneca
Falls

Troy

nger Lakes

Cayuga Lake

Cortland

Cooperstown

Albany ★

M A S S A C H U S E T T S

N E W · Y O R K

Keuka
Lake

FINGER
LAKES N.F.

Ithaca

Oneonta

Susquehanna

Catskill

Hudson

Bath

Watkins Glen

A P P A L A C H I A N

Catskill

Hudson

Corning

W. Br. Delaware

Mountains

Elmira

Endwell

Binghamton

CATSKILL
PARK

Slide Mt.
+ 4,180 ft
1,274 m

Kingston

Taconic Ranges

LVANIA

Susquehanna

E. Branch Delaware

M O U N T A I N S

Chemung

New Paltz

Beacon

Poughkeepsie

TRAIL

CONNECTICUT

▲ Standing in New York Harbor, the Statue of Liberty, a gift from the people of France, is a symbol of freedom and democracy.

RHODE
ISLAND

Newburgh

◀ Once seriously polluted, the Gowanus Canal in New York City's borough of Brooklyn has been undergoing cleaning efforts. Here, people canoe and enjoy the view from the water.

Middletown

Port
Jervis

Delaware

APPALACHIAN

NATIONAL

SCENIC

Peekskill

New City

Tarrytown

Spring Valley

White Plains

Yonkers

New Rochelle

Huntington

Long Island
Sound

Block Island
Sound

Montauk
Point

East Hampton

Centereach

Southampton

Map Key

★ State capital

•• City or town

····· Boundary

▨ Indian Reservation

▨ State Park

▨ National Recreation Area
National Seashore

▨ National Forest

▨ National Wildlife Refuge

New York

Ellis Island —

NEW
JERSEY

Staten
Island

GATEWAY
N.R.A.

Brentwood

Levittown

FIRE ISLAND
NATIONAL
SEASHORE

Freeport

Long Beach

L o n g   I s l a n d

ATLANTIC
OCEAN

N

0   50 miles

0   75 kilometers

The Northeast

Pennsylvania

 Land & Water The Allegheny Mountains, the Pocono Mountains, and the Susquehanna River are important land and water features of Pennsylvania.

 Statehood Pennsylvania became the 2nd state in 1787.

People & Places Pennsylvania's population is 12,448,279. Harrisburg is the state capital. The largest city is Philadelphia.

Fun Fact The town of Hershey is known as the Chocolate Capital of the World. The Hershey Company exports its chocolate candies to more than 90 countries around the world.

Pennsylvania State Flag

Mountain Laurel State Flower

Ruffed Grouse State Bird

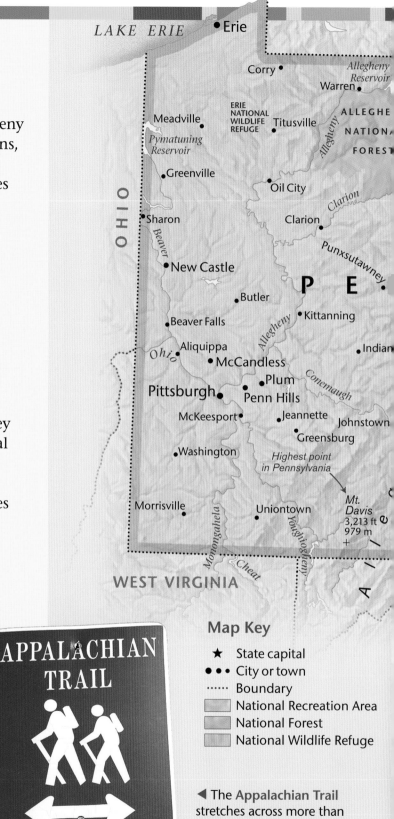

LAKE ERIE • Erie

Corry •

Warren •

Allegheny Reservoir

Meadville •

ERIE NATIONAL WILDLIFE REFUGE

Titusville •

ALLEGHE

NATIONA

FOREST

Pymatuning Reservoir

• Greenville

• Oil City

Clarion

• Sharon

Clarion •

Beaver

OHIO

• New Castle

Punxsutawney •

P   E

• Butler

Kittanning •

• Beaver Falls

Allegheny

• Indian

Ohio

Aliquippa •

• McCandless

Conemaugh

Pittsburgh •

• Plum

• Penn Hills

McKeesport •

• Jeannette

Johnstown

Greensburg

• Washington

Highest point in Pennsylvania

Mt. Davis 3,213 ft 979 m

Morrisville •

Uniontown •

Monongahela

Cheat

Youghiogheny

A l l e ... e

WEST VIRGINIA

Map Key

★ State capital
••• City or town
...... Boundary
National Recreation Area
National Forest
National Wildlife Refuge

APPALACHIAN TRAIL

◀ The **Appalachian Trail** stretches across more than 2,000 miles (3,200 km) from Maine to Georgia. The trail passes through 14 states, including Pennsylvania.

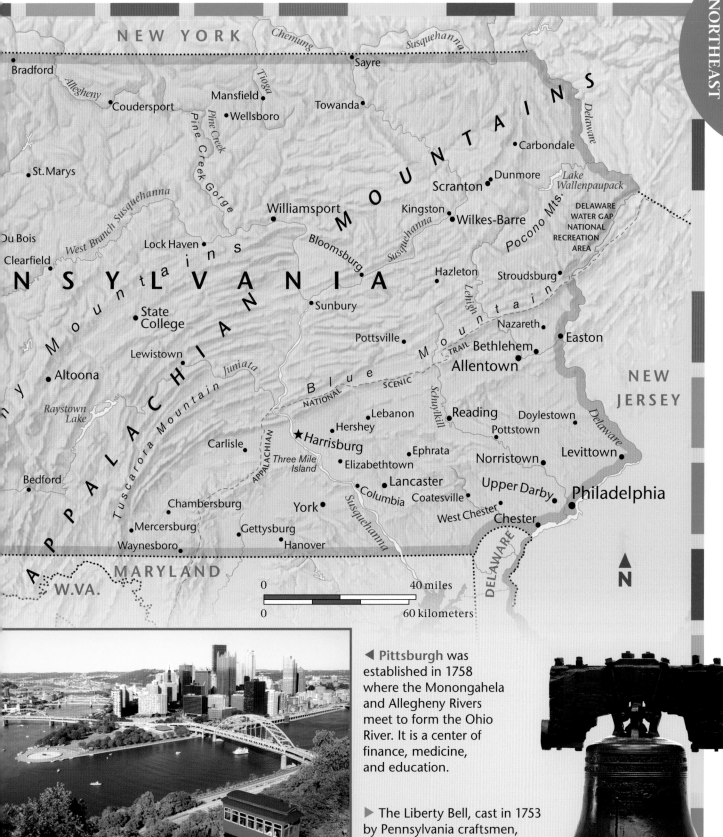

NEW YORK

Chemung

Susquehanna

Bradford

Allegheny

Coudersport

Mansfield

Tioga

Sayre

Towanda

Wellsboro

Pine Creek

Pine Creek Gorge

Carbondale

St.Marys

Dunmore

Scranton

Lake Wallenpaupack

Williamsport

West Branch Susquehanna

Kingston

Wilkes-Barre

MOUNTAINS

Delaware

Du Bois

Lock Haven

Bloomsburg

Susquehanna

Pocono Mts.

DELAWARE WATER GAP NATIONAL RECREATION AREA

Clearfield

Hazleton

Stroudsburg

NSYLVANIA

Mountains

Sunbury

Nazareth

Lehigh

Mountain

State College

Pottsville

TRAIL

Bethlehem

Easton

Lewistown

Blue

SCENIC

Allentown

NEW JERSEY

Altoona

Juniata

NATIONAL

Mountain

Schuylkill

Lebanon

Reading

Doylestown

Delaware

Raystown Lake

APPALACHIAN

Tuscarora Mountain

Hershey

Pottstown

Carlisle

Harrisburg

Ephrata

Norristown

Levittown

Three Mile Island

Elizabethtown

Bedford

APPALACHIAN

Lancaster

Upper Darby

Philadelphia

Columbia

Coatesville

Chambersburg

York

Susquehanna

West Chester

Chester

Mercersburg

Gettysburg

DELAWARE

Waynesboro

Hanover

A.

MARYLAND

W.VA.

0   40 miles

0   60 kilometers

N

◀ **Pittsburgh** was established in 1758 where the Monongahela and Allegheny Rivers meet to form the Ohio River. It is a center of finance, medicine, and education.

▶ The Liberty Bell, cast in 1753 by Pennsylvania craftsmen, hangs in Philadelphia. Because of a crack, it is no longer rung.

Rhode Island

Land & Water Block Island and Narragansett Bay, with its many islands, are important land and water features of Rhode Island.

Statehood Rhode Island became the 13th state in 1790.

People & Places Rhode Island's population is 1,050,788. Providence is the state capital and the largest city.

Fun Fact Rhode Island is the smallest state in size in the United States. It measures just 48 miles from north to south and 37 miles from east to west.

▲ Sailing is a popular sport in Rhode Island. This boat is in full sail on a late summer day on Narragansett Bay.

◀ The North Lighthouse on the northern tip of Block Island still warns ships of dangerous waters. The building, constructed in 1867, is not a typical lighthouse design.

Rhode Island State Flag

Violet
State Flower

Rhode Island Red
State Bird

▼ Rhode Island has cold, snowy winters. Skaters bundled in warm clothing enjoy ice skating on the City Center public rink in Providence.

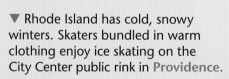

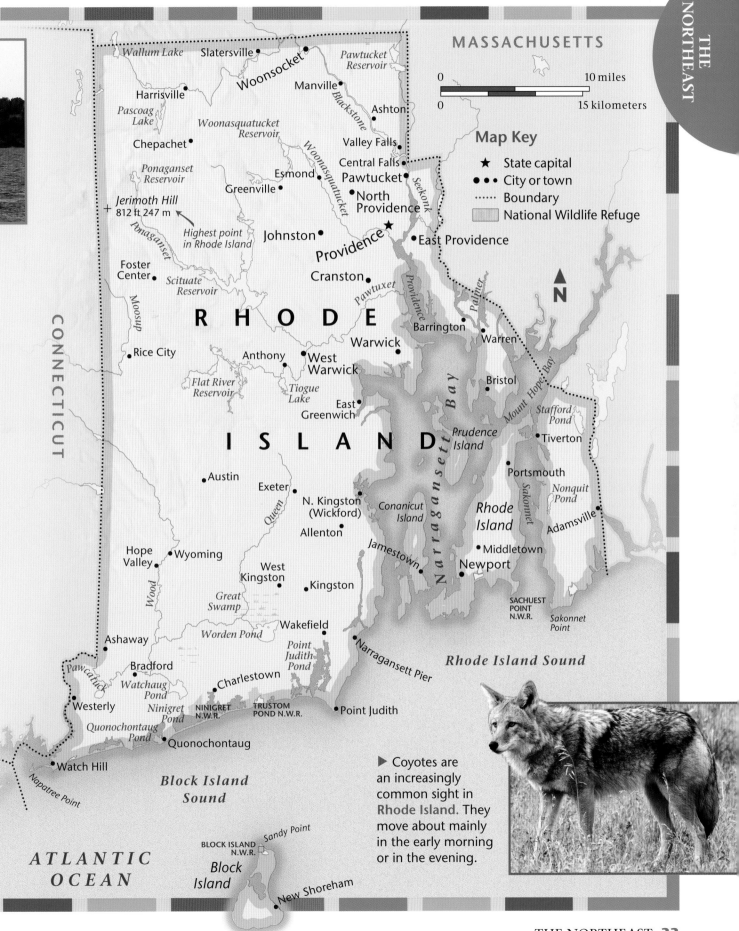

MASSACHUSETTS

Wallum Lake
Slatersville
Woonsocket
Pawtucket Reservoir
Harrisville
Manville
Ashton
Pascoag Lake
Woonasquatucket Reservoir
Blackstone
Chepachet
Valley Falls
Ponaganset Reservoir
Esmond
Central Falls
Woonasquatucket
Pawtucket
Greenville
North Providence
Seekonk
+ Jerimoth Hill
812 ft 247 m
Ponaganset
Highest point in Rhode Island
Johnston
Providence
East Providence

Foster Center
Scituate Reservoir
Cranston
Moosup
Pawtuxet
Barrington
Palmer
Warren

R H O D E

Rice City
Anthony
Warwick
Bristol
West Warwick
Flat River Reservoir
Tiogue Lake
East Greenwich

I S L A N D

Austin
Exeter
N. Kingston (Wickford)
Conanicut Island
Prudence Island
Stafford Pond
Tiverton
Allenton
Portsmouth
Nonquit Pond
Queen
Rhode Island
Adamsville
Hope Valley
Wyoming
Jamestown
Middletown
Newport
West Kingston
Kingston
Great Swamp
Wood
Wakefield
SACHUEST POINT N.W.R.
Sakonnet Point
Ashaway
Worden Pond
Narragansett Pier
Rhode Island Sound
Bradford
Pawcatuck
Point Judith Pond
Watchaug Pond
Charlestown
Westerly
Ninigret Pond
NINIGRET N.W.R.
TRUSTOM POND N.W.R.
Point Judith
Quonochontaug Pond
Quonochontaug
Watch Hill
Napatree Point
Block Island Sound

Narragansett Bay
Mount Hope Bay
Sakonnet
Providence

CONNECTICUT

Map Key
★ State capital
• • • City or town
⋯⋯ Boundary
▨ National Wildlife Refuge

0   10 miles
0   15 kilometers

N

▶ Coyotes are an increasingly common sight in Rhode Island. They move about mainly in the early morning or in the evening.

ATLANTIC OCEAN
BLOCK ISLAND N.W.R.
Sandy Point
Block Island
New Shoreham
Block Island Sound

Vermont

Land & Water The Green Mountains, Lake Champlain, and the Connecticut River are important land and water features of Vermont.

Statehood Vermont became the 14th state in 1791.

People & Places Vermont's population is 621,270. Montpelier is the state capital. The largest city is Burlington.

Fun Fact From the end of the Revolutionary War until 1791, Vermont was an independent republic with its own government and money. It even thought about uniting with Canada.

Vermont State Flag

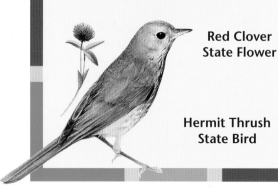

Red Clover
State Flower

Hermit Thrush
State Bird

▲ Vermont ice cream is famous worldwide. The headquarters of Ben & Jerry's in Burlington is the number one tourist attraction in the state.

▲ People collect the sap of maple trees, which is boiled to make maple sugar and syrup. Maple production is celebrated each year at a festival in Tunbridge.

QUEBEC

CANADA
U.S.

MISSISQUOI
N.W.R.

Richford

Lake
Memphremagog

Derby Center

Canaan

North Hero
Island

Saint Albans

Fairfield

Missisquoi

Newport

Clyde

Seymour
Lake

Island Pond

Connecticut

South Hero
Island

Lamoille

Barton

Lake
Willoughby

Lake
Champlain

Mt. Mansfield
4,393 ft
1,339 m

Morrisville

Passumpsic

Moose

Essex
Junction

Highest point
in Vermont

Burlington

South Burlington

Stowe

St. Johnsbury

Shelburne

Winooski

Waterbury

Moore
Reservoir

NEW
HAMPSHIRE

Map Key

★ State capital

• • • City or town

• • • • Boundary

National Recreation Area

National Forest

National Wildlife Refuge

LONG TRAIL

Montpelier

Mad

Barre

Vergennes

Graniteville

Wells River

GREEN

Middlebury

V E R M O N T

MOUNTAIN

Lake
Dunmore

Randolph

Otter Creek

White

Tunbridge

Bradford

NATIONAL

APPALACHIAN MOUNTAINS

▶ With as much as
100 inches (254 cm)
of snow each
winter, Vermont's
Green Mountains
provide plenty of
opportunities for
snowboarding
and skiing.

Brandon

Lake
Bomoseen

FOREST

APPALACHIAN

NATIONAL

SCENIC

TRAIL

Proctor

Poultney

Hartford

Fair
Haven

Rutland

+ Killington Peak
4,235 ft 1,291 m

Poultney

Windsor

NEW YORK

Ludlow

Black

WHITE ROCKS NATIONAL
RECREATION AREA

Springfield

Mettawee

GREEN

Batten Kill

MOUNTAIN

Stratton Mt.
3,936 ft
1,200 m

Bellows Falls

▼ Farming has a long history in Vermont.
The state produces dairy products, fruits and
vegetables, maple syrup, and Christmas trees.

Arlington

NATIONAL

Somerset
Reservoir

West

Hoosic

+ Mt. Snow
3,556 ft
1,084 m

Putney

FOREST

Taconic

Range

(LONG TRAIL)

Bennington

Deerfield

Brattleboro

Connecticut

Pownal
Center

Harriman
Reservoir

M A S S A C H U S E T T S

0 ———————— 40 miles

0 ———————— 60 kilometers

N

The Southeast

The Southeast region of the United States is full of variety, both in its landscape and in its history. The Appalachian Mountains are old and worn down. The coastal margins are marked by barrier islands and wetlands. And in the western part of the region, the Mississippi River flows out through a broad delta. The region, with roots in agriculture, suffered great destruction during the Civil War, but today it is a part of the Sunbelt, where cities are growing rapidly and the economy is shifting to high-tech industries.

Live oak trees, some hundreds of years old, form a natural arch across a country road in Georgia. These trees, draped in Spanish moss, are common in the coastal Southeast. Flamingoes are a familiar sight in parks in Florida.

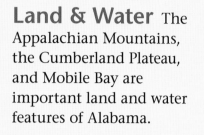

The Southeast

Alabama

Land & Water The Appalachian Mountains, the Cumberland Plateau, and Mobile Bay are important land and water features of Alabama.

Statehood Alabama became the 22nd state in 1819.

People & Places Alabama's population is 4,661,900. Montgomery is the state capital. The largest city is Birmingham.

Fun Fact The world's youngest college graduate earned a bachelor's degree in anthropology from the University of South Alabama when he was just 10 years and four months old.

▲ Southern Alabama has a narrow coastline fronting the Gulf of Mexico. The beach resort of **Gulf Shores** is a popular tourist destination.

▲ A welder repairs a boat in **Bayou La Batre** on Alabama's Gulf coast. The town is a center for shipbuilding and seafood processing.

▼ This old railroad bridge, built in 1839, was a toll bridge across the **Tennessee River**. Today it is a pedestrian bridge.

Alabama State Flag

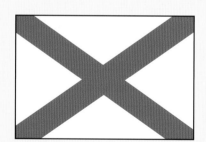

Northern Flicker State Bird

Camellia State Flower

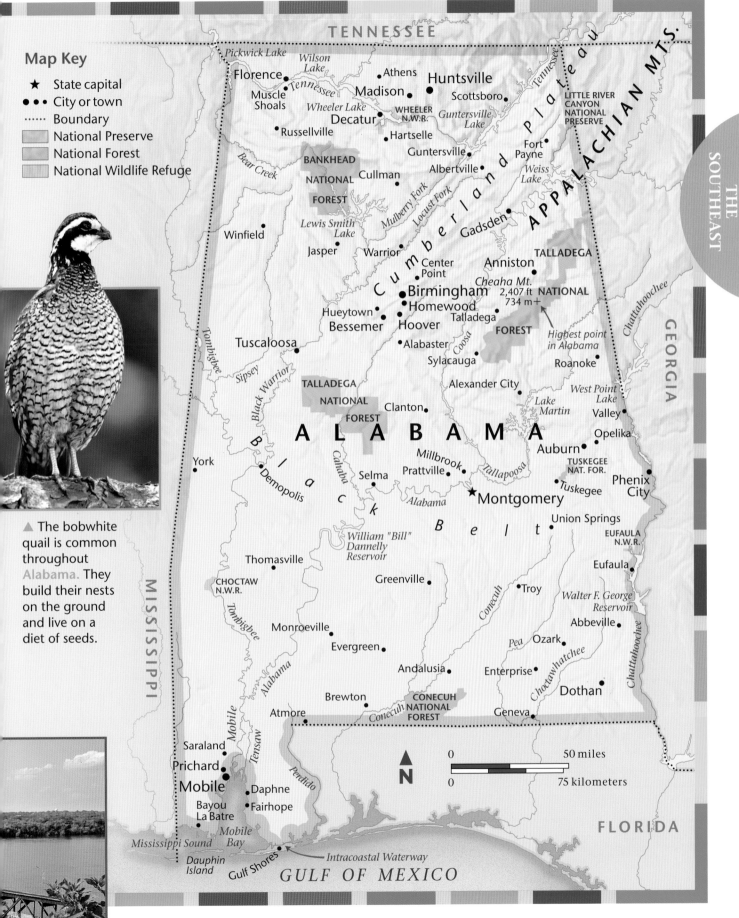

Map Key

★ State capital
••• City or town
····· Boundary
National Preserve
National Forest
National Wildlife Refuge

▲ The bobwhite quail is common throughout Alabama. They build their nests on the ground and live on a diet of seeds.

TENNESSEE

Pickwick Lake
Wilson Lake
Florence
Tennessee
Muscle Shoals
Athens
Madison
Huntsville
Scottsboro
Wheeler Lake
WHEELER N.W.R.
Decatur
Guntersville Lake
Russellville
Hartselle
LITTLE RIVER CANYON NATIONAL PRESERVE
Guntersville
BANKHEAD NATIONAL FOREST
Cullman
Albertville
Fort Payne
Weiss Lake
Bear Creek
Lewis Smith Lake
Winfield
Mulberry Fork
Locust Fork
Gadsden
APPALACHIAN MTS.
Jasper
Warrior
Center Point
Anniston
TALLADEGA
Cheaha Mt.
2,407 ft
734 m+
NATIONAL
Birmingham
Homewood
Hueytown
Bessemer
Hoover
Talladega
FOREST
Highest point in Alabama
Tuscaloosa
Alabaster
Sipsey
Coosa
Sylacauga
Roanoke
Tombigbee
Black Warrior
TALLADEGA NATIONAL FOREST
Alexander City
West Point Lake
Lake Martin
Valley
York
Clanton
A L A B A M A
Opelika
Cahaba
Millbrook
Prattville
Auburn
Demopolis
Selma
Tallapoosa
TUSKEGEE NAT. FOR.
Phenix City
B l a c k
Alabama
Montgomery
Tuskegee
B e l t
Union Springs
William "Bill" Dannelly Reservoir
EUFAULA N.W.R.
CHOCTAW N.W.R.
Thomasville
Greenville
Troy
Eufaula
Walter F. George Reservoir
Conecuh
Abbeville
Monroeville
Tombigbee
Pea
Ozark
Choctawhatchee
Evergreen
Andalusia
Enterprise
Dothan
Alabama
Brewton
CONECUH NATIONAL FOREST
Geneva
Conecuh
Chattahoochee
Atmore
GEORGIA
Chattahoochee
MISSISSIPPI
Saraland
Mobile
Prichard
Tensaw
Mobile
Daphne
Perdido
Bayou La Batre
Fairhope
FLORIDA
Mississippi Sound
Mobile Bay
Dauphin Island
Gulf Shores
Intracoastal Waterway
GULF OF MEXICO

N

0   50 miles
0   75 kilometers

Arkansas

 Land & Water The Ouachita Mountains, the Ozark Plateau, and the Mississippi River are important land and water features of Arkansas.

Statehood Arkansas became the 25th state in 1836.

People & Places Arkansas's population is 2,855,390. Little Rock is the state capital and the largest city.

 Fun Fact Crater of Diamonds State Park near Murfreesboro yielded the largest natural diamond ever found in the United States in 1924. The stone, called "Uncle Sam," weighed more than 40 carats.

◀ A student with his laptop computer sits on the monument to Confederate soldiers on the state capitol grounds in **Little Rock**.

Arkansas State Flag

**Apple Blossom
State Flower**

**Mockingbird
State Bird**

▲ A farmer in **eastern Arkansas** checks the progress of his rice crop. The state is a leading producer of rice.

MISSOURI

Bentonville
Rogers
Siloam Springs
Berryville
Beaver Lake
Springdale
Harrison
Mountain Home

OZARK N.F.
Fayetteville

Boston Mountains

OZARK NATIONAL FOREST

Bull Shoals Lake
Norfork Lake

White

Buffalo
BUFFALO NATIONAL RIVER

Mountain View

OZARK NATIONAL FOREST

Corning

Pocahontas

Paragould

BIG LAKE N.W.R.

Jonesboro
Blytheville

Batesville

Tuckerman
Trumann

Newport
Marked Tree

Spring

Black

White

Mississippi

TENNESSEE

THE SOUTHEAST

Van Buren
Ozark
Lake Dardanelle
Fort Smith

Highest point in Arkansas
OZARK N.F.
+ Magazine Mt.
2,753 ft
839 m

Mulberry
Arkansas
Big Piney Cr.
Russellville
Morrilton
HOLLA BEND N.W.R.

Clinton

Greers Ferry Lake

Heber Springs

Searcy

Conway
Cabot

Little Red

Wynne

L'Anguille

Cache

St. Francis

West Memphis

Forrest City

CACHE RIVER NAT. WILDLIFE REF.

A R K A N S A S

Waldron

OUACHITA NATIONAL

Ouachita Mountains FOREST

Mena

Lake Ouachita

Hot Springs

De Gray Lake

Jacksonville
North Little Rock
Little Rock ★

Benton

Malvern
Sheridan

Stuttgart

Brinkley

ST. FRANCIS NATIONAL FOREST
West Helena
Helena

MISSISSIPPI

N

Cossatot

Lake Greeson

Murfreesboro
CRATER OF DIAMONDS S.P.

DeQueen

COSSATOT N.W.R.

Little

Little Missouri

Millwood Lake

Ashdown

Prescott

Hope

TEXAS

Texarkana

Stamps

Magnolia

Lake Erling

Arkadelphia

Saline

White Oak Lake

Camden

Ouachita

El Dorado

Red

Pine Bluff

Arkansas

Bayou Bartholomew

Fordyce

Monticello

Warren

Dermott

FELSENTHAL N.W.R.

Hamburg

Crossett

Lake Jack Lee

Dumas

WHITE RIVER NATIONAL WILDLIFE REFUGE

White

Mississippi

OVERFLOW N.W.R.

Map Key

★ State capital
••• City or town
····· Boundary
State Park
National Park
National Forest
National Wildlife Refuge

0   50 miles
0   75 kilometers

LOUISIANA

◀ The White River flows through the Ozark Plateau. Its cold water is a perfect habitat for trout, a popular sport fish.

Jenkins Fishing Service

The Southeast

Florida

Land & Water The Florida Keys, the Everglades, and Lake Okeechobee are important land and water features of Florida.

Statehood Florida became the 27th state in 1845.

People & Places Florida's population is 18,328,340. Tallahassee is the state capital. The largest city is Jacksonville.

Fun Fact Everglades National Park is home to rare and endangered species such as the American crocodile, the Florida panther, and the West Indian manatee.

Florida State Flag

Orange Blossom State Flower

Mockingbird State Bird

A L A B A M A

Highest point in Florida → ＋ Britton Hill 345 ft 105 m

Perdido

Crestview

Fort Walton Beach

Pensacola

Choctawhatchee

GULF ISLANDS NATIONAL SEASHORE

Panan City

Intracoastal Waterway

▼ The manatee is the state marine mammal of **Florida.** It averages 10 feet (3 m) in length and can weigh 1,000 pounds (450 kg).

▼ **Kennedy Space Center** on Florida's Atlantic coast has been the launch site for all U.S. human space flight missions.

▲ Two young boys adjust their snorkels before exploring the warm waters near John Pennecamp Park in the **Florida Keys.**

▼ **Orange County,** in central Florida, is a major producer of citrus fruit. Florida is the leading producer in the U.S.

The Southeast

Georgia

Land & Water

The Blue Ridge Mountains, the Okefenokee Swamp, and the Savannah River are important land and water features of Georgia.

Statehood
Georgia became the 4th state in 1788.

People & Places

Georgia's population is 9,685,744. Atlanta is the state capital and the largest city.

Fun Fact
The Georgia Aquarium in Atlanta is the largest aquarium in the world. It features more than 100,000 animals living in more than 8 million gallons (30.3 million liters) of water.

◀ Built for the 1996 Olympic Games, Centennial Olympic Park in **Atlanta** is the site of festivals and community events that attract an estimated 3 million visitors each year.

▶ Nearly half the peanut crop in the United States is grown in Georgia. **Sylvester** is the peanut capital of the world.

Georgia State Flag

Cherokee Rose
State Flower

Brown Thrasher
State Bird

▼ A Great Grey Heron surveys its surroundings from its perch in a tree in the **Okefenokee National Wildlife Refuge** in southeastern Georgia.

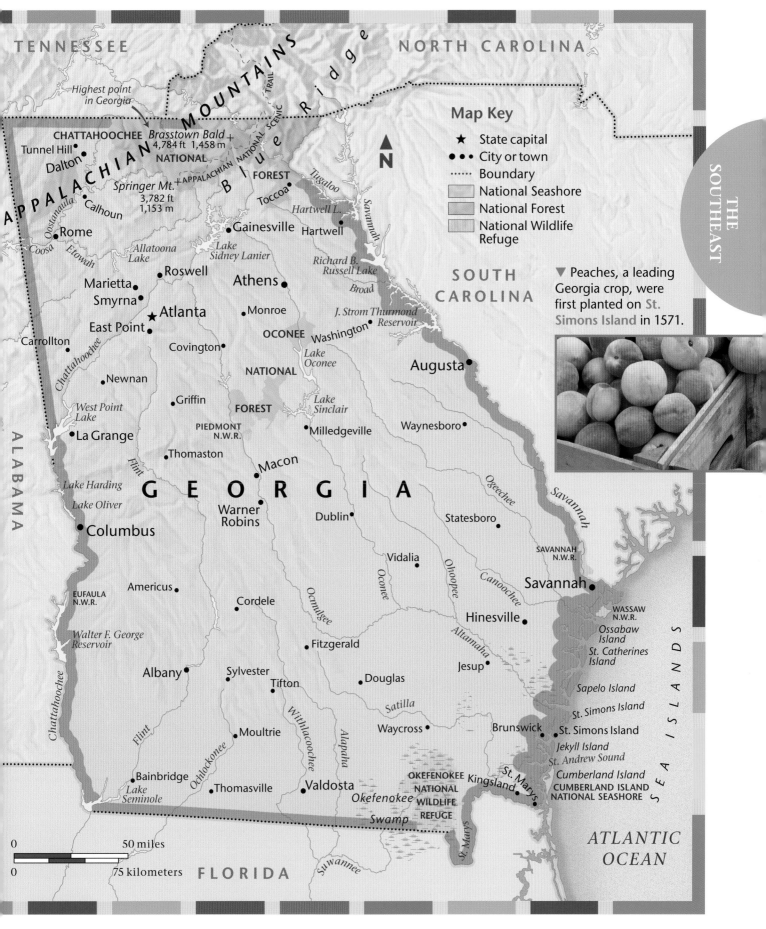

TENNESSEE

NORTH CAROLINA

Highest point in Georgia

CHATTAHOOCHEE
Tunnel Hill
Dalton
NATIONAL

Brasstown Bald
4,784 ft 1,458 m

APPALACHIAN NATIONAL SCENIC
TRAIL

Tugaloo

FOREST

Springer Mt.
3,782 ft
1,153 m

APPALACHIAN
MOUNTAINS

Blue Ridge

Toccoa

Hartwell L.

Savannah

Hartwell

Oostanaula
Calhoun
Rome
Coosa
Etowah

Allatoona Lake

Lake Sidney Lanier

Gainesville

Richard B.
Russell Lake

Broad

Map Key

★ State capital
• • • City or town
• • • • Boundary
National Seashore
National Forest
National Wildlife Refuge

N

Marietta
Smyrna
Atlanta
East Point

Roswell

Athens

Monroe

J. Strom Thurmond Reservoir

SOUTH
CAROLINA

Carrollton

Covington

Chattahoochee

OCONEE

Washington

▼ Peaches, a leading Georgia crop, were first planted on **St. Simons Island** in 1571.

Newnan

Griffin

NATIONAL

Lake Oconee

Augusta

West Point
Lake

PIEDMONT
N.W.R.

FOREST

Lake Sinclair

Waynesboro

La Grange

Thomaston

Milledgeville

Macon

GEORGIA

Lake Harding
Lake Oliver

Warner
Robins

Dublin

Statesboro

Ogeechee

Savannah

Columbus

Flint

SAVANNAH
N.W.R.

Vidalia

Oconee

Ohoopee

Canoochee

Savannah

Americus

EUFAULA
N.W.R.

Cordele

WASSAW
N.W.R.

Hinesville

Ossabaw Island

Walter F. George Reservoir

Fitzgerald

Ocmulgee

Altamaha

Jesup

St. Catherines Island

Albany
Sylvester
Tifton

Douglas

Satilla

Sapelo Island

Chattahoochee

Moultrie

Withlacoochee

Alapaha

Waycross

Brunswick

St. Simons Island

St. Simons Island

Jekyll Island

St. Andrew Sound

Flint

Ochlockonee

Bainbridge

Thomasville

Valdosta

OKEFENOKEE

Kingsland

Cumberland Island

CUMBERLAND ISLAND
NATIONAL SEASHORE

Lake Seminole

NATIONAL

WILDLIFE

St. Marys

Okefenokee Swamp

REFUGE

0   50 miles

0   75 kilometers

FLORIDA

St. Marys

Suwannee

ATLANTIC
OCEAN

S E A   I S L A N D S

ALABAMA

Kentucky

Land & Water Mammoth Cave, Cumberland Plateau, and the Ohio River are important land and water features of Kentucky.

Statehood Kentucky became the 15th state in 1792.

People & Places Kentucky's population is 4,269,245. Frankfort is the state capital. The largest city is Louisville.

Fun Fact The song "Happy Birthday to You," one of the most popular songs in the English language, was written in 1893 by two sisters living in Louisville.

▶ Shaker Village in **Pleasant Hill** preserves the culture and history of this important social movement.

◀ Abraham Lincoln, 16th President, was born near **Hodgenville**. His profile appears on the penny.

IN GOD WE TRUST
LIBERTY
2006
D

ILLINOIS

Wabash

Henderson

Marion
Madisonville

Ohio
Cumberland
Tradewater
Princeton

Paducah
Calvert City
Kentucky Lake
Hopkinsville

MISSOURI
Mayfield
LAND BETWEEN THE LAKES NAT. REC. AREA
Lake Barkley
Little

Mississippi
Mayfield
Creek

Fulton
Murray
Cumberland
Tennessee

REELFOOT N.W.R.

▼ The setting sun turns the sky red over **Cave Run Lake**. The lake is a popular vacation spot because of its natural beauty.

Kentucky State Flag

Goldenrod State Flower

Cardinal State Bird

Map Key

★ State capital
• • • City or town
∙∙∙∙∙∙ Boundary
National Park
National Recreation Area
National Forest
National Wildlife Refuge

0 ━━━━━━ 50 miles
0 ━━━━━━ 75 kilometers

N

OHIO

INDIANA

Covington • Newport
Florence
Ohio
Licking
Williamstown
Maysville • Vanceburg
North Fork
Ashland
Ohio
Kentucky
Eagle Creek
South Fork
Cynthiana
Flemingsburg

B L U E G R A S S
La Grange
Shelbyville
Jeffersontown
Frankfort ★
Georgetown
Lexington
Paris
Licking
Morehead
Cave Run Lake
Mt. Sterling
Winchester
DANIEL
WEST VIRGINIA
Little Sandy
Big Sandy
Levisa Fork
Tug Fork

Louisville
Brandenburg
R E G I O N
Salt
Kentucky
Red
BOONE
Prestonsburg
Owensboro
Radcliff
Bardstown
Pleasant Hill
Harrodsburg
Richmond
North Fork
Middle Fork
Jackson
Pikeville
Rough River Lake
Elizabethtown
Hodgenville
Danville
Berea
NATIONAL
S. Fk.
Hazard

Ohio
K E N T U C K Y
Rough
Leitchfield
Nolin River Lake
Campbellsville
Rolling Fork
Mount Vernon
Kentucky
Rockcastle
Highest point in Kentucky
Cumberland
Jefferson
VIRGINIA NATIONAL
Green
MAMMOTH CAVE NATIONAL PARK
Cave City
Green River Lake
Somerset
London
FOREST
Black Mt.
4,145 ft
1,263 m
Pine Mountain
Cumberland
FOREST
Bowling Green
Glasgow
Corbin
Barren
Barren River Lake
Cumberland
Lake Cumberland
Cumberland Mts.
APPALACHIAN
Franklin
CUMBERLAND GAP N.H.P.
Middlesboro
Cumberland Gap
MOUNTAINS
Albany
Dale Hollow Lake
BIG SOUTH FORK NAT. RIVER & REC. AREA

TENNESSEE

◀ Riders in colorful jerseys astride powerful race horses charge out of the starting gate during a race in Kentucky. The state is a major producer of thoroughbred race horses.

The Southeast

Louisiana

 Land & Water Driskill Mountain, Lake Pontchartrain, and the Mississippi River are important land and water features of Louisiana.

Statehood Louisiana became the 18th state in 1812.

 People & Places Louisiana's population is 4,410,796. Baton Rouge is the state capital and the largest city.

Fun Fact The Louisiana State Capitol building in Baton Rouge is the tallest of all the state capitols. It is a limestone skyscraper that stands 450 feet (137 m) tall and has 34 stories!

Louisiana State Flag

Magnolia State Flower

Brown Pelican State Bird

▲ Musicians practice on a park bench in **New Orleans** as they wait for one of the city's Mardi Gras parades to begin.

▲ The *Mississippi Queen,* a paddle wheel boat, churns up the water as it steams along the Mississippi River between **Baton Rouge** and New Orleans.

Springhill KISATC
Caddo Lake   NATION
Bossier City   FOREST
Minden
Shreveport   Lake Bistine
Red
Mansfield   Red
Toledo Bend Reservoir   Natchitoche
Many
Leesville
TEXAS
De Ridder
Sabine
De Quinc
Lake Charles
Sulphur
Intracoastal CAMER
Caleasieu   PRA N.V
Lake
Sabine Lake   SABINE NAT. WILDLIFE REFUGE

◄ Louisiana produces almost half the shrimp caught in the U.S. Most of it comes from the **Barataria-Terrebonne** estuary of the Mississippi River.

ARKANSAS

UPPER
OUACHITA
N.W.R.

Lake
Providence

Bastrop

Bayou D'Arbonne

D'ARBONNE
N.W.R.

Ruston

West
Monroe

Monroe

Tallulah

Driskill Mt.
535 ft
163 m

*Highest point
in Louisiana*

TENSAS
RIVER
N.W.R.

Jonesboro

Winnsboro

SATCHIE

Ferriday

Winnfield

CATAHOULA
N.W.R.

*Catahoula
Lake*

ATIONAL

Alexandria

Pineville

LAKE
OPHELIA
N.W.R.

REST

Marksville

MISSISSIPPI

L O U I S I A N A

Oakdale

Zachary

Amite

Bogalusa

▶ A colorful mask decorated with ribbons is a reminder of Mardi Gras, which is celebrated in **Louisiana** in late winter each year.

▲ The Caddo Black Bayou Preserve (near Caddo Lake), a natural wetland with hardwood forest, cypress swamps, and rare plant species, is a protected area that is closed to the public.

Map Key

★ State capital
••• City or town
····· Boundary
National Forest
National Wildlife Refuge

BOGUE
CHITTO
N.W.R.

Opelousas

ATCHAFALAYA
N.W.R.

Hammond

Baton Rouge

Eunice

Mandeville

Slidell

nnings

Breaux Bridge

Gonzales

*Lake
Maurepas*

*Lake
Pontchartrain*

Mississippi Sound

Crowley

Lafayette

BAYOU SAUVAGE N.W.R.

 CASSINE
W.R.

New Iberia

Donaldsonville

Kenner

Metairie

Lake Borgne

*Chandeleur
Sound*

Chandeleur
Islands

Waterway

Abbeville

New Orleans

Chalmette

*Grand
Lake*

Avery Island

Franklin

Thibodaux

*Lake
Salvador*

BRETON

NATIONAL

*White
Lake*

Morgan City

*Breton
Sound*

WILDLIFE

Houma

Larose

REFUGE

*Breton
Islands*

*Marsh
Island*

*Atchafalaya
Bay*

Port Sulphur

*Barataria
Bay*

DELTA N.W.R.

GULF OF MEXICO

Grand Isle

*Mississippi
River Delta*

0   50 miles
0   75 kilometers

N

Mississippi

Land & Water The Mississippi Petrified Forest, the Tennessee-Tombigbee Waterway, and the Mississippi River are important land and water features of Mississippi.

Statehood Mississippi became the 20th state in 1817.

People & Places Mississippi's population is 2,938,618. Jackson is the state capital and the largest city.

Fun Fact Jim Henson, creator of Kermit the Frog, Miss Piggy, Big Bird, and other famous Muppets, was born in Greenville.

▲ Mississippi is the leading producer of catfish in the U.S. A part of the Mississippi River valley known as the Delta is the main producing area.

▲ Two bridges stretch across the Mississippi River in the town of Vicksburg. The river is home to more than 400 species of wildlife.

▼ Children play in a tidal pool on a Biloxi beach as the sun sets. Barrier islands separate the city from the Gulf of Mexico.

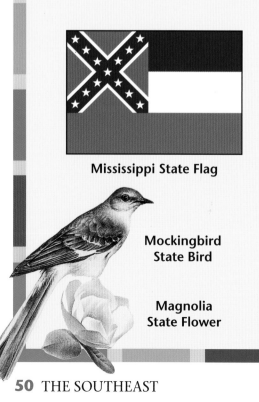

Mississippi State Flag

Mockingbird State Bird

Magnolia State Flower

▲ Farmers in **Mississippi** plant more than a million acres (405,000 ha) of cotton each year. Technology and improved seeds keep production high.

Map Key

★ State capital
• • • City or town
• • • • • Boundary
▢ Indian Reservation
▢ State Park
▢ National Seashore
▢ National Forest
▢ National Wildlife Refuge

ARKANSAS

Mississippi

Southaven
Arkabutla Lake
Holly Springs
HOLLY SPRINGS
Corinth
Pickwick Lake
Tennessee
Woodall Mt.
806 ft 246 m
NATIONAL
Ripley
Booneville
TISHOMINGO S.P.
Senatobia
Sardis Lake
FOREST
Baldwyn
New Albany
Highest point in Mississippi

Coldwater

Batesville
Oxford
Little Tallahatchie
Pontotoc
Tupelo
Fulton

Clarksdale
Enid Lake
Yocona
Water Valley
TOMBIGBEE NAT. FOR.
Okolona
Amory

TALLAHATCHIE NAT. WILDLIFE REFUGE
Tallahatchie
HOLLY SPRINGS N.F.
Houston
Aberdeen

Shelby
Big Sunflower

Ruleville
Grenada Lake
Yalobusha
West Point

Cleveland
Grenada
Starkville
Columbus

DAHOMEY N.W.R.
Greenwood
Winona
TOMBIGBEE NATIONAL FOREST
NOXUBEE N.W.R.

D E L T A
Leland
Indianola
Tombigbee

Greenville
MORGAN BRAKE N.W.R.
Big Black
Kosciusko
Louisville
Noxubee

Hollandale
HILLSIDE N.W.R.

YAZOO N.W.R.
Yazoo

PANTHER SWAMP N.W.R.
MISSISSIPPI
Philadelphia
MISSISSIPPI CHOCTAW INDIAN RESERVATION

DELTA NATIONAL FOREST
Yazoo City
Carthage

MISSISSIPPI PETRIFIED FOREST
Canton
Pearl
Okatibbee Lake

Mississippi
Ross Barnett Reservoir
Meridian

Deer Creek
Ridgeland
BIENVILLE
Forest
Newton

Clinton
Pearl
NATIONAL FOREST

Vicksburg
★ **Jackson**
Brandon
Strong

Yazoo
Leaf
Quitman
ALABAMA

Crystal Springs
Magee
Tallahala
Chickasawhay

Hazlehurst
Laurel
Waynesboro

HOMOCHITTO
Collins
Ellisville
Creek

NATIONAL
Brookhaven
Pearl
DE SOTO

Natchez
ST. CATHERINE CREEK N.W.R.
FOREST
Petal

Homochitto
McComb
Columbia
Hattiesburg

Centreville
Bogue Chitto
NATIONAL

LOUISIANA
Poplarville
Lucedale
Black Creek

Mississippi
BOGUE CHITTO N.W.R.
Wiggins
FOREST
Pascagoula

⊛ N
Picayune
Ocean Springs
Gulfport
Biloxi
MISSISSIPPI SANDHILL CRANE N.W.R.
Moss Point

Long Beach
Pascagoula

0 ___ 50 miles
Bay St. Louis
Mississippi Sound

0 ___ 75 kilometers
GULF ISLANDS NAT. SEASHORE
GULF OF MEXICO

North Carolina

Land & Water Mount Mitchell, the Outer Banks, and the Cape Fear River are important land and water features of North Carolina.

Statehood North Carolina became the 12th state in 1789.

People & Places North Carolina's population is 9,222,414. Raleigh is the state capital. The largest city is Charlotte.

Fun Fact The University of North Carolina, the first public university in the U. S., opened its doors in 1795 with 2 professors and 41 students.

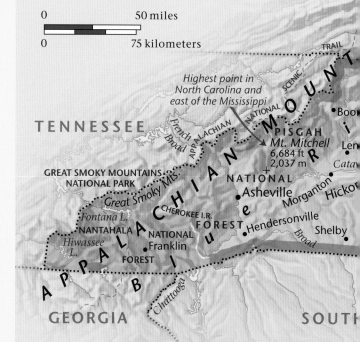

TENNESSEE

Highest point in North Carolina and east of the Mississippi

GREAT SMOKY MOUNTAINS NATIONAL PARK

Great Smoky Mts.

Fontana L.

NANTAHALA

Hiwassee L.

Franklin

NATIONAL

FOREST

CHEROKEE I.R.

APPALACHIAN

BLue

FOREST

GEORGIA

Chattooga

APPALACHIAN

SCENIC

TRAIL

French Broad

PISGAH

Mt. Mitchell
6,684 ft
2,037 m

NATIONAL

Asheville

Morganton

Hendersonville

Boo

Len

Cata

Hickor

Shelby

Broad

SOUTH

North Carolina State Flag

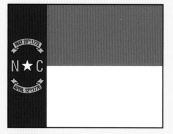

Cardinal State Bird

Flowering Dogwood State Flower

▲ The chapel tower is a landmark on the campus of Duke University in **Durham.**

◀ Basketball is a popular sport among all ages in **North Carolina,** whether on the court or in the backyard.

VIRGINIA

Mt. Airy •   Eden •   *Dan*   John H. Kerr   *Lake*   • Roanoke Rapids
Reidsville •   Roxboro •   Reservoir   *Gaston*

GREAT
DISMAL
SWAMP
N.W.R.

*Great
Dismal
Swamp*

MACKAY ISLAND N.W.R.

Yadkin   Greensboro •   *Haw*   Henderson   *Roanoke*   Elizabeth • City

Kitty Hawk

Winston-Salem •   Burlington •   *Falls L.*   Rocky   Edenton

Albemarle Sound   Roanoke Island

High Point •   Chapel Hill •   Durham •   Mount

ALLIGATOR
RIVER
N.W.R.

*Hatteras
Island*

tesville   Lexington •   B.Everett   ★ Raleigh   Williamston •

POCOSIN
LAKES
N.W.R.

CAPE
HATTERAS
NATIONAL
SEASHORE

*Lake
Norman*   Salisbury •   Asheboro •   Jordan • Cary • Garner   Wilson •

Tar

N O R T H   C A R O L I N A

MATTAMUSKEET
N.W.R.

Outer Banks

nnapolis •   Concord •   UWHARRIE   Sanford •   Goldsboro •

SWANQUARTER
N.W.R.

Pamlico Sound

Gastonia •   Albemarle •   NATIONAL   FOREST   Dunn •   Kinston •

Neuse

Ocracoke
Island

Cape Hatteras

Charlotte •   PEE DEE   Pinehurst •   Clinton •   New Bern •

Neuse R.

CEDAR ISLAND
N.W.R.

Monroe •   N.W.R.   Fayetteville •   Jacksonville •

CROATAN
NAT.
FOREST   • Havelock

Raleigh Bay

CAPE
LOOKOUT
NATIONAL
SEASHORE

Laurinburg •   *Lumber*   *South*

AROLINA   *Pee Dee*   Lumberton •

Morehead
City

ATLANTIC
OCEAN

Onslow Bay   Cape Lookout

Whiteville •   *Lake
Waccamaw*   Wilmington •

*Green
Swamp*   Wrightsville
Beach

Cape Fear

Intracoastal Waterway   • Southport

Long Bay   Cape Fear

Map Key

★   State capital
• • •   City or town
· · · · ·   Boundary
    Indian Reservation
    National Park
    National Seashore
    National Forest
    National Wildlife Refuge

◀ Cape Lookout Lighthouse on the **Outer Banks** has warned ships of dangerous sandbars since it began operation in 1812.

▶ Orville and Wilbur Wright, from Dayton, Ohio, made the first successful airplane flight near **Kitty Hawk** on North Carolina's Outer Banks.

South Carolina

Land & Water The Blue Ridge Mountains, Lake Marion, and the Cooper River are important land and water features of South Carolina.

Statehood South Carolina became the 8th state in 1788.

People & Places South Carolina's population is 4,479,800. Columbia is the state capital and the largest city.

Fun Fact Sweetgrass baskets have been made in the coastal lowland region for more than 300 years. They were originally used in the planting and processing of rice.

Map details:
- *Highest point South Carolina* Sassafras Mt. 3,560 ft 1,085 m
- SUMTER NATIONAL FOREST
- *Chattooga*, *Tugaloo*, *Savannah*
- Lake Keowee, Hartwell Lake
- Easley, Seneca, Clemson, Simpsonville, Greenville, Green, Laurer, Anderson
- Greenwood, Richard B. Russell Lake, SUMTER
- J. Strom Thurmo Reservoir, NATIONAL
- FORE, Nor Augus
- GEORGIA

Map Key

- ★ State capital
- ••• City or town
- ...... Boundary
- National Park
- National Forest
- National Wildlife Refuge

0 ————— 50 miles
0 ————— 75 kilometers

▼ Large container ships carrying valuable manufactured goods link South Carolina to the global economy. **Charleston** is the state's largest port.

South Carolina State Flag

Yellow Jessamine
State Flower

Carolina Wren
State Bird

NORTH CAROLINA

Gaffney
Wylie Lake
Spartanburg
York
Rock Hill
Union
Chester
Lancaster
Cheraw
Broad
Catawba
SUMTER
CAROLINA
SANDHILLS
N.W.R.

NATIONAL
FOREST
Wateree Lake
Hartsville
Dillon
Great Pee Dee
Winnsboro
Darlington
Newberry
Florence
Marion
Loris
Wateree
Lake Murray
Saluda
Irmo
S O U T H
Lynches
Conway
Intracoastal Waterway
West Columbia
★ Columbia
Sumter
Lake City
Cayce
Congaree
Myrtle Beach
gefield
CONGAREE
NATIONAL PARK
Little Pee Dee
Garden City

C A R O L I N A
Aiken
Orangeburg
N. Fork Edisto
S. Fork Edisto
Black
Georgetown
Long Bay
Williston
Lake Marion
Great Pee Dee
Bamberg
Edisto
Lake Moultrie
Santee
North Island
Moncks Corner
FRANCIS
MARION
NATIONAL
FOREST
Cape Island
A T L A N T I C
Savannah
Allendale
Cooper
Summerville
Hanahan
CAPE
ROMAIN
N.W.R.
O C E A N
N
Walterboro
Combahee
North
Charleston
Charleston
Mount
Pleasant
Coosawhatchie
Edisto Island
Beaufort
St. Helena Sound
St. Helena Island
SAVANNAH
NATIONAL
WILDLIFE
REFUGE
Parris Island
Port Royal Sound
Hilton Head Island
Hilton Head Island
Daufuskie Island
S E A I S L A N D S

▲ Alligators are native to swamps and streams of South Carolina. They are especially common in the coastal area known as the **Lowcountry**.

▼ Hard-packed sands on a **Hilton Head Island** beach are perfect for a family bicycle outing.

Tennessee

Land & Water The Appalachian Mountains, Reelfoot Lake, and the Tennessee River are important land and water features of Tennessee.

Statehood Tennessee became the 16th state in 1796.

People & Places Tennessee's population is 6,214,888. Nashville is the state capital. The largest city is Memphis.

Fun Fact Graceland, Elvis Presley's colonial-style 23-room mansion and estate in Memphis, was declared a National Historic Landmark in 2006. It is the second most visited house in the country.

Tennessee State Flag

Iris
State Flower

Mockingbird
State Bird

MISSOURI

Kentucky Lake
LAND BETWEEN
THE LAKES
NATIONAL REC. AREA

Mississippi

REELFOOT
N.W.R.
Reelfoot L.
• Union City
• Martin
Paris •
TENNESSEE

Obion
• Dyersburg
NATIONAL

ARKANSAS
CHICKASAW
N.W.R.
WILDLIFE

REFUGE

LOWER HATCHIE
N.W.R.
Brownsville
•
• Jackson

HATCHIE
N.W.R.
• Millington
Hatchie
Savannah •

Mississippi
• Bartlett
Germantown
• Collierville
Pickwick
Lake

Memphis
Tenne

MISSISSIPPI

▶ **Memphis** is famous for its barbecue, especially baby back ribs that are cooked so long that the meat falls from the bones.

▼ Norris Dam, on a tributary of the **Tennessee River**, was completed in 1936. It was constructed to generate electricity.

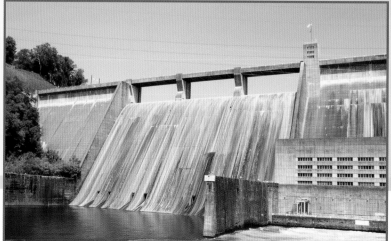

KENTUCKY

VIRGINIA

0   50 miles
0   75 kilometers

rkley

SS CREEKS
J.R.

Red   Springfield
Clarksville   Gallatin
Goodlettsville   Old Hickory L.

ckson

Nashville ★   Hendersonville   Lebanon
Brentwood   Cookeville
Franklin   Center Hill
Smyrna   J. Percy   Lake   Sparta
Priest Lake

Columbia   Murfreesboro   McMinnville
Lewisburg   Shelbyville
falo   Tullahoma
Pulaski   Tims Ford
Lake
Elk

Dale Hollow
Lake

BIG SOUTH FORK
NATIONAL RIVER AND
RECREATION AREA

Cumberland

Cumberland   Plateau

Obed

Caney Fork

Chickamauga Lake

Sequatchie

Tennessee

Cumberland

Chattanooga
Red Bank   Soddy
Daisy
East Ridge

Norris Lake   Powell   CUMBERLAND
GAP N.H.P.

Clinch

Knoxville   Douglas Lake
Oak Ridge   Sevierville
Fort Loudoun
Watts   Lake   Gatlinburg
Bar
Lake   Maryville
Tellico
Lake   CHEROKEE
Athens   NATIONAL
Cleveland
FOREST   Hiwassee

Kingsport   Elizabethton   Bristol
Holston   Johnson City
Greeneville
Morristown   Cherokee
Lake   CHEROKEE
Newport   SCENIC
FOREST   NATIONAL   NATIONAL

Great   Smoky Mts.   APPALACHIAN
APPALACHIAN   MOUNTAINS

+ Clingmans Dome
6,643 ft 2,025 m

GREAT SMOKY
MOUNTAINS
NATIONAL PARK

Highest point
in Tennessee

TENNESSEE

French
Broad

TRAIL

Nolichucky

NORTH
CAROLINA

ALABAMA   GEORGIA   SOUTH
CAROLINA

Map Key

★ State capital
••• City or town
····· Boundary
▨ National Park
National Recreation Area
▨ National Forest
▨ National Wildlife Refuge

N

▲ The Grand Ole Opry in Nashville is the home of
country music. Country music performers mainly use
stringed instruments. The music form evolved from
traditional folk tunes of the Appalachians.

◄ A male whitetail deer with a full rack of antlers watches for
danger in a meadow in the Great Smoky Mountains National
Park. The park is a popular vacation destination.

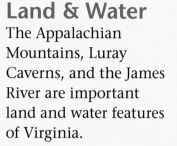

Virginia

Land & Water

The Appalachian Mountains, Luray Caverns, and the James River are important land and water features of Virginia.

Statehood
Virginia became the 10th state in 1788.

People & Places
Virginia's population is 7,769,089. Richmond is the state capital. The largest city is Virginia Beach.

Fun Fact
Eight U.S. Presidents—Washington, Jefferson, Madison, Monroe, Harrison, Tyler, Taylor, and Wilson—were born in Virginia, more than any other state.

▲ An old barn, bales of hay, and trees in autumn foliage are a common sight in the **Appalachian Mountains** of Virginia.

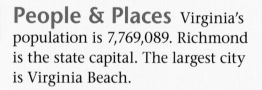

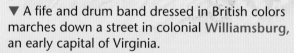

▼ A fife and drum band dressed in British colors marches down a street in colonial **Williamsburg**, an early capital of Virginia.

Virginia State Flag

Flowering Dogwood State Flower

Cardinal State Bird

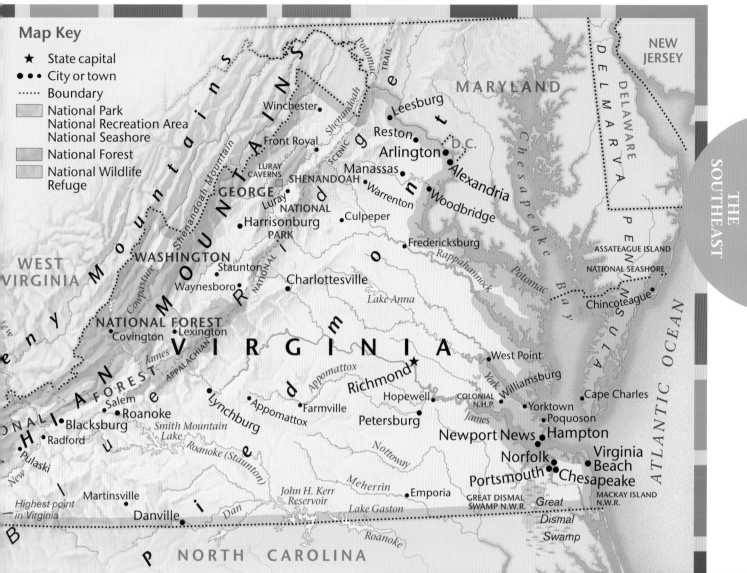

Map Key

- ★ State capital
- • • • City or town
- ‥‥‥ Boundary
- National Park
  National Recreation Area
  National Seashore
- National Forest
- National Wildlife Refuge

MARYLAND

NEW JERSEY

DELAWARE

DELMARVA PENINSULA

POTOMAC TRAIL

Winchester

Leesburg

Reston

Shenandoah

Front Royal

LURAY CAVERNS

SHENANDOAH

GEORGE

Luray

NATIONAL

Harrisonburg

PARK

D.C.

Arlington

Manassas

Alexandria

Warrenton

Woodbridge

Culpeper

Fredericksburg

Rappahannock

Chesapeake Bay

ASSATEAGUE ISLAND
NATIONAL SEASHORE

Potomac

Chincoteague

WEST VIRGINIA

WASHINGTON

Staunton

NATIONAL

Waynesboro

Charlottesville

Lake Anna

Cowpasture

NATIONAL FOREST

Covington

Lexington

APPALACHIAN

James

V I R G I N I A

West Point

York

Williamsburg

Cape Charles

ATLANTIC OCEAN

FOREST

Salem

Roanoke

Blacksburg

Radford

Appomattox

Richmond

Appomattox

Farmville

Hopewell

COLONIAL
N.H.P.

Yorktown

Poquoson

Lynchburg

Petersburg

James

Newport News

Hampton

Smith Mountain Lake

Roanoke (Staunton)

Norfolk

Virginia Beach

Pulaski

Nottoway

Portsmouth

Chesapeake

New

Meherrin

MACKAY ISLAND
N.W.R.

Highest point in Virginia

Martinsville

John H. Kerr Reservoir

Emporia

GREAT DISMAL
SWAMP N.W.R.

Great

Danville

Dan

Lake Gaston

Dismal

B

Roanoke

Swamp

P

NORTH CAROLINA

ALLEGHENY Mountains

Shenandoah Mountain

MOUNTAINS

NATIONAL

BLUE RIDGE

APPALACHIAN

▶ Winding under the Appalachian Mountains, Luray Caverns formed as water dissolved rocks and the minerals dripped down to form stalactites and stalagmites.

◀ The sharp eyes of a Great Blue Heron watch the water of a river near Richmond for a dinner of fish or frogs.

West Virginia

Land & Water The Allegheny Mountains, Elk River, and the New River are important land and water features of West Virginia.

Statehood West Virginia became the 35th state in 1863.

People & Places West Virginia's population is 1,814,468. Charleston is the state capital and the largest city.

Fun Fact One of the oldest and largest Indian burial grounds is located in Moundsville. It is more than 2,000 years old and 69 feet (21 m) high.

▲ West Virginia's rivers offer some of the best whitewater rafting in the eastern U.S. The **Gauley River** is called the Beast of the East.

◄ A coal miner's helmet recalls the history of mining in **West Virginia**. The state produced 13 percent of U.S. coal in 2006.

▼ Trees turn red in the **Dolly Sods Wilderness** in the Monongahela National Forest. The area is named for an early settler family.

Point Pleasant

Kan...

Ohio

Hurrican...

Huntington

Big Sandy

Guyandotte

Tug Fork

Logan

Williamson

KENTUCKY

West Virginia State Flag

Rhododendron
State Flower

Cardinal
State Bird

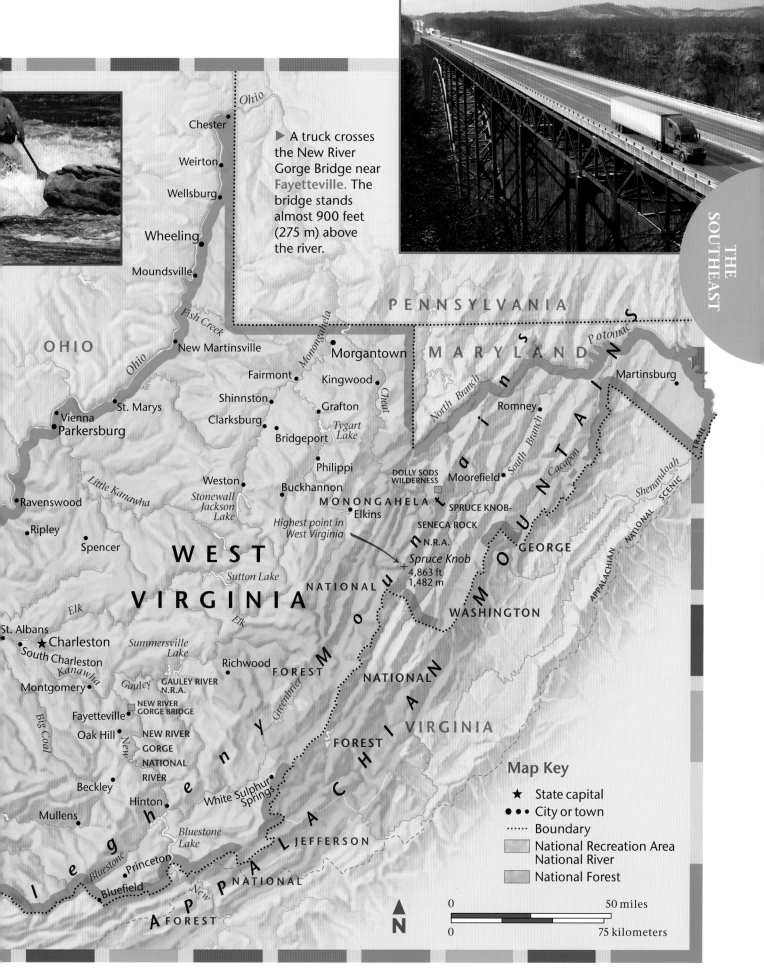

A truck crosses the New River Gorge Bridge near **Fayetteville**. The bridge stands almost 900 feet (275 m) above the river.

PENNSYLVANIA

OHIO

Chester
Weirton
Wellsburg
Wheeling
Moundsville

Ohio

Fish Creek

New Martinsville

Ohio

Vienna
Parkersburg

St. Marys

Ravenswood

Ripley

Spencer

Little Kanawha

**WEST
VIRGINIA**

Weston

Stonewall Jackson Lake

Sutton Lake

Elk

Elk

St. Albans
★ Charleston
South Charleston

Kanawha

Montgomery

Big Coal

Fayetteville

Oak Hill

NEW RIVER GORGE BRIDGE

NEW RIVER GORGE NATIONAL RIVER

New

Beckley

Hinton

Mullens

Bluestone

Bluestone Lake

Princeton

Bluefield

New

NATIONAL

A FOREST

Clarksburg
Shinnston
Fairmont
Bridgeport

Philippi
Buckhannon

Tygart Lake

Grafton

Kingwood

Morgantown

Monongahela

Cheat

MARYLAND

North Branch

Potomac

Romney

Moorefield

South Branch

Cacapon

Martinsburg

DOLLY SODS WILDERNESS

MONONGAHELA

Elkins

Highest point in West Virginia

**SPRUCE KNOB-SENECA ROCK
N.R.A.**

Spruce Knob
4,863 ft
1,482 m

NATIONAL

Mountains

FOREST

NATIONAL

FOREST

GEORGE

WASHINGTON

Appalachian

Shenandoah

NATIONAL SCENIC TRAIL

VIRGINIA

Richwood

GAULEY RIVER N.R.A.

Gauley

Greenbrier

White Sulphur Springs

JEFFERSON

Map Key

★ State capital
••• City or town
········ Boundary
▮ National Recreation Area National River
▮ National Forest

0 — 50 miles
0 — 75 kilometers

N

The Midwest

The Midwest is a region of glacier-carved lakes, mighty rivers, and rolling prairies. The Great Lakes are among the largest freshwater lakes in the world. The Mississippi River and its tributaries—the Missouri and the Ohio Rivers—drain America's heartland. The region's lowlands and plains support some of the most productive agriculture in the world. Industries such as food processing, steel, and automobile production supported the growth of cities such as Pittsburgh, Chicago, and St. Louis, but they are being replaced by businesses based on technology and information.

The setting sun turns this Kansas prairie a golden red. The Midwest is a major grain-producing region. Dairy cows are also an important part of the region's economy, supplying much of the country's milk, cheese, and butter.

Illinois

Land & Water

The Shawnee National Forest, the Illinois River, and Lake Michigan are important land and water features of Illinois.

Statehood
Illinois became the 21st state in 1818.

People & Places

Illinois's population is 12,901,563. Springfield is the state capital. The largest city is Chicago.

Fun Fact
The Chicago River is dyed green on St. Patrick's Day to honor the city's large Irish population. The formula for the green dye is a closely kept secret.

◄ Children ride bicycles along a sidewalk in Pilsen, on **Chicago**'s lower west side. A street mural provides a clue to the neighborhood's immigrant population.

▲ Pig races are a fun-filled highlight of the annual **Illinois** State Fair in Springfield.

ILLINOIS

Illinois State Flag

**Violet
State Flower**

**Cardinal
State Bird**

WRIGLEY FIELD
HOME OF
CHICAGO CUBS

PIRATES	TOP 9TH	CUBS
1		4

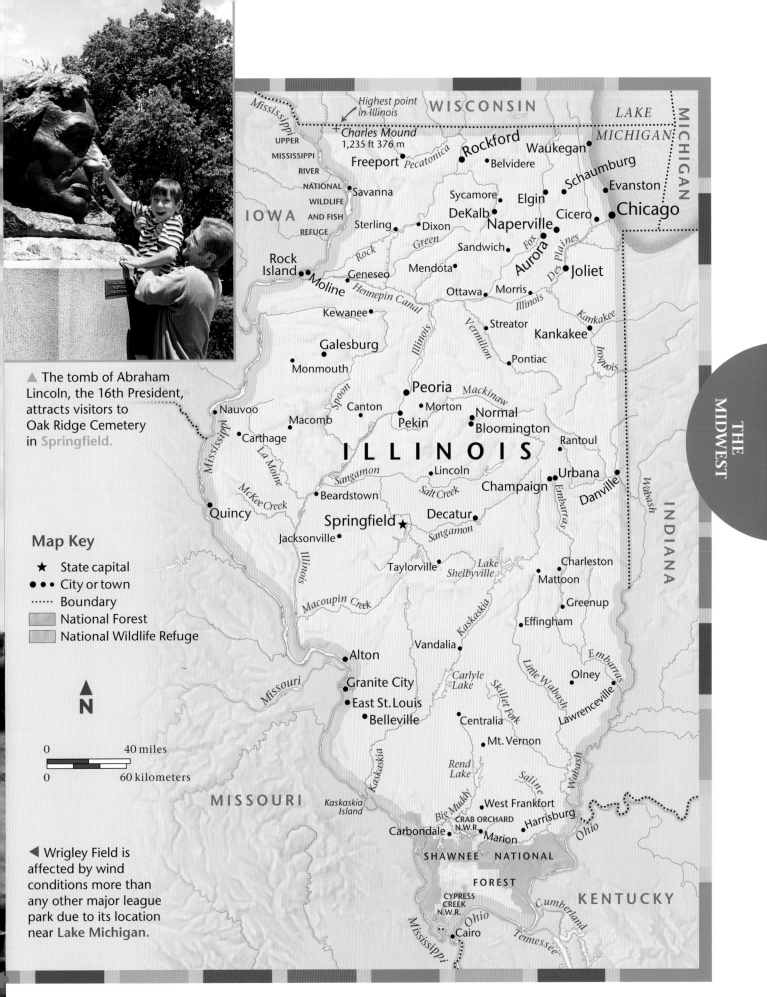

The tomb of Abraham Lincoln, the 16th President, attracts visitors to Oak Ridge Cemetery in Springfield.

Map Key

★ State capital
• • • City or town
· · · · · Boundary
National Forest
National Wildlife Refuge

N

0   40 miles
0   60 kilometers

◄ Wrigley Field is affected by wind conditions more than any other major league park due to its location near Lake Michigan.

Highest point in Illinois
+ Charles Mound
1,235 ft 376 m

WISCONSIN

LAKE MICHIGAN

MICHIGAN

Mississippi

UPPER MISSISSIPPI RIVER NATIONAL WILDLIFE AND FISH REFUGE

IOWA

Savanna

Freeport   Pecatonica   Rockford   Waukegan

Belvidere

Sycamore   Elgin   Schaumburg   Evanston

DeKalb   Cicero   Chicago

Sterling   Dixon   Naperville

Green

Rock

Sandwich   Fox   Aurora   Des Plaines

Rock Island   Geneseo

Moline

Hennepin Canal

Mendota   Joliet

Ottawa   Morris

Illinois

Kewanee

Streator   Kankakee

Galesburg

Monmouth

Spoon

Canton   Morton

Peoria   Mackinaw

Pekin   Normal   Bloomington

Vermilion

Pontiac

Kankakee   Iroquois

Rantoul

ILLINOIS

Nauvoo

Macomb

Carthage

La Moine

Sangamon   Lincoln   Urbana

Salt Creek   Champaign   Danville

Embarras

Wabash

INDIANA

McKee Creek

Quincy

Beardstown

Springfield ★   Decatur

Sangamon

Jacksonville

Taylorville   Lake Shelbyville   Charleston

Mattoon

Illinois

Greenup

Macoupin Creek   Kaskaskia   Effingham

Vandalia

Alton   Carlyle Lake   Olney

Missouri

Granite City   Skillet Fork   Little Wabash   Lawrenceville

East St. Louis

Belleville   Centralia   Embarras

Kaskaskia   Mt. Vernon

Rend Lake   Saline   Wabash

MISSOURI

Kaskaskia Island   Big Muddy   West Frankfort

CRAB ORCHARD N.W.R.   Harrisburg

Carbondale   Marion   Ohio

SHAWNEE NATIONAL

FOREST

CYPRESS CREEK N.W.R.   Ohio   Cumberland   KENTUCKY

Mississippi   Cairo   Tennessee

The Midwest

Iowa

Land & Water
Hawkeye Point and the Missouri and Mississippi Rivers are important land and water features of Iowa.

Statehood
Iowa became the 29th state in 1846.

People & Places
Iowa's population is 3,002,555. Des Moines is the state capital and the largest city.

Fun Fact
Iowa's nickname, the Hawkeye State, comes from chief Black Hawk, a Sauk Indian chief who started the Black Hawk War in 1832.

▲ Hogs outnumber people five to one in Iowa, which produces 25 percent of all hogs raised in the U.S.

Iowa State Flag

Wild Rose
State Flower

American
Goldfinch
State Bird

SOUTH DAKOTA

Hawkeye Point +
1,670 ft
509 m

Highest point
in Iowa

Big Sioux

• Sheldon

• Orange City

Le Mars •

Floyd

Cherokee •

Missouri

• Sioux City

Little Sioux

• Onawa

Denise

NEBRASKA

Boyer

Harla

DE SOTO N.W.R.

• Council Bluffs

• Glenwoo

Missouri

• Shenandoa

Map Key
★ State capital
••• City or town
····· Boundary
▨ National Wildlife Refuge

◀ A young boy dressed in a colorful traditional outfit prepares to participate in the Annual Meskwaki Indian Powwow near Tama, Iowa.

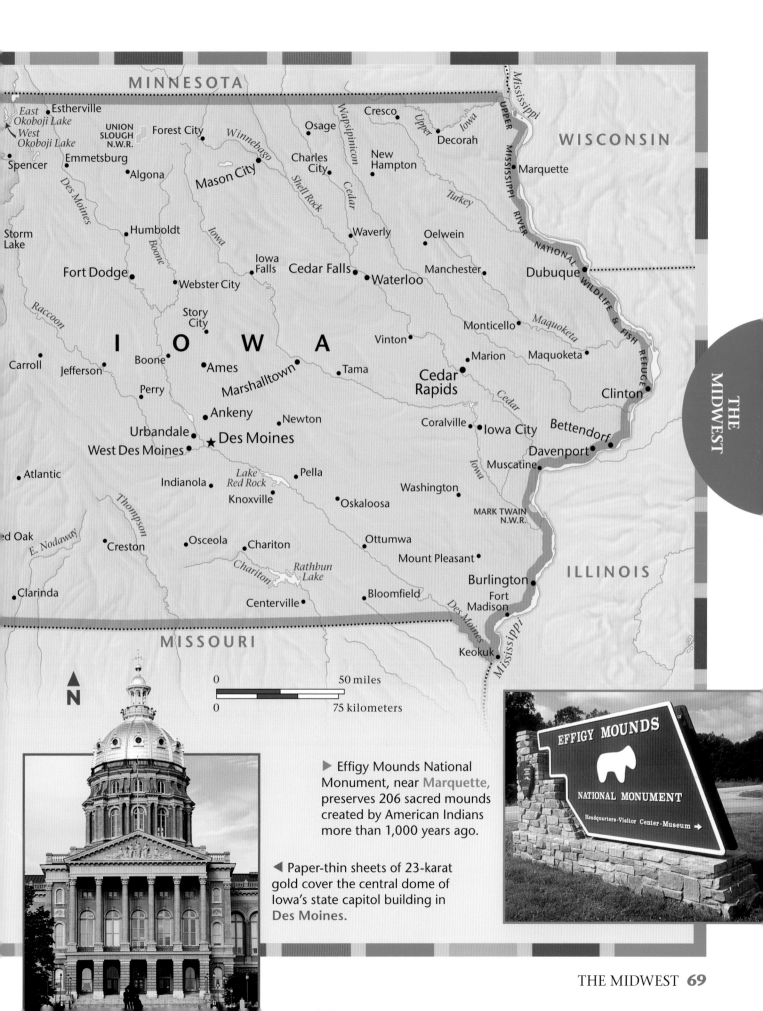

MINNESOTA

WISCONSIN

East Okoboji Lake
West Okoboji Lake
Esterville
Spencer
Emmetsburg
UNION SLOUGH N.W.R.
Forest City
Algona
Winnebago
Osage
Cresco
Wapsipinicon
Upper Iowa
Decorah
Marquette

Charles City
New Hampton
Des Moines
Mason City
Humboldt
Shell Rock
Cedar
Waverly
Oelwein
Turkey

Storm Lake
Fort Dodge
Boone
Webster City
Iowa Falls
Cedar Falls
Waterloo
Manchester
Dubuque

Story City
Iowa
Vinton
Monticello
Maquoketa

I O W A

Carroll
Jefferson
Boone
Ames
Marshalltown
Tama
Marion
Maquoketa

Raccoon
Perry
Cedar Rapids
Cedar
Clinton

Ankeny
Newton
Coralville
Iowa City
Bettendorf

Urbandale
★ Des Moines
West Des Moines
Davenport
Muscatine

Atlantic
Indianola
Lake Red Rock
Pella
Washington
Iowa

Knoxville
Oskaloosa
MARK TWAIN N.W.R.

Thompson
ed Oak
Creston
Osceola
Chariton
Ottumwa
Mount Pleasant

E. Nodaway
Chariton
Rathbun Lake
Bloomfield
Burlington
ILLINOIS

Clarinda
Centerville
Fort Madison
Des Moines
Keokuk
Mississippi

MISSOURI

UPPER MISSISSIPPI RIVER NATIONAL WILDLIFE & FISH REFUGE

THE MIDWEST

N

0 ___ 50 miles
0 ___ 75 kilometers

▶ Effigy Mounds National Monument, near Marquette, preserves 206 sacred mounds created by American Indians more than 1,000 years ago.

◀ Paper-thin sheets of 23-karat gold cover the central dome of Iowa's state capitol building in Des Moines.

EFFIGY MOUNDS
NATIONAL MONUMENT
Headquarters-Visitor Center-Museum ➤

Kansas

Land & Water Mount Sunflower, the Flint Hills, and the Missouri River are important land and water features of Kansas.

Statehood Kansas became the 34th state in 1861.

People & Places The population of Kansas is 2,802,134. Topeka is the state capital. The largest city is Wichita.

Fun Fact Pizza Hut, the world's largest pizza chain, opened its first restaurant in Wichita in 1958. Today the company has branches in more than 100 countries.

▲ A statue of the Tin Man, a character from the popular 1939 fantasy movie *The Wizard of Oz*, which was set in Kansas, sits in a garden.

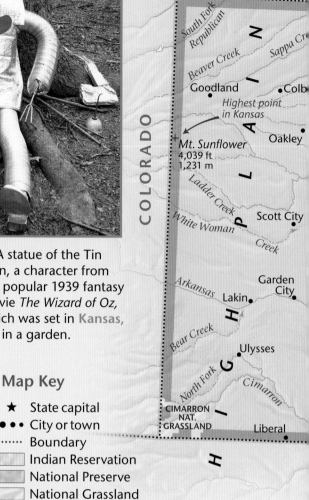

Map Key

★ State capital
●●● City or town
······ Boundary
Indian Reservation
National Preserve
National Grassland
National Wildlife Refuge

▼ The Chalk Pyramids are located in Gove County south of Oakley. These limestone formations were carved by erosion from the floor of an ancient inland sea.

KANSAS

Kansas State Flag

Sunflower State Flower

Western Meadowlark State Bird

NEBRASKA

Norton
Phillipsburg
Kirwin Reservoir
Lebanon
Belleville
Washington
Little Blue
Seneca
SAC AND FOX I.R.
IOWA I.R.
Missouri
Hiawatha
irie Dog Creek
Big Blue
Marysville
KICKAPOO INDIAN RESERVATION
KIRWIN N.W.R.
North Fork Solomon
Waconda Lake
Concordia
Republican
Clay Center
Tuttle Creek Lake
Holton
POTAWATOMI INDIAN RESERVATION
Atchison
Leavenworth
South Fork Solomon
Beloit
Solomon
Manhattan
Wamego
Perry Lake
Kansas City
Missouri
Plainville
Minneapolis
Milford Lake
Topeka ★
Overland Park
S m o k y   H i l l s
Kansas
WaKeeney
Wilson Lake
Saline
Junction City
Lawrence
Olathe
Cedar Bluff Reservoir
Hays
Russell
Abilene
Salina
Smoky Hill
Council Grove
Osage City
Ottawa
Hillsdale Lake
Smoky Hill
Ellsworth
Kanopolis Lake

K A N S A S
Cheyenne Bottoms
McPherson
Neosho
Emporia
Osawatomie
Marais des Cygnes
Ness City
Walnut Creek
Great Bend
Lyons
TALLGRASS PRAIRIE NATIONAL PRESERVE
John Redmond Reservoir
Garnett
Pawnee
Arkansas
Larned
QUIVIRA N.W.R.
Marion Lake
Hesston
FLINT HILLS N.W.R.
Burlington
Buckner Creek
Newton
Verdigris
Iola
Kinsley
Hutchinson
El Dorado Lake
Eureka
Fort Scott
odge City
Cheney Reservoir
Wichita
El Dorado
Flint Hills
Fall
Chanute
Neosho
Pittsburg
Greensburg
Pratt
Kingman
Derby
Fredonia
Elk City Lake
R e d   H i l l s
Medicine Lodge
Medicine Lodge
Mulvane
Walnut
Elk
Parsons
Meade
Crooked Creek
Wellington
Winfield
Independence
Baxter Springs
Cimarron
Anthony
Arkansas City
Caney
Coffeyville
Arkansas

OKLAHOMA

N

0   50 miles
0   75 kilometers

MISSOURI

◄ People in carts and covered wagons reenact the westward movement through Kansas of traders and early settlers along the Santa Fe Trail following the Missouri and upper Arkansas Rivers towards Colorado and New Mexico.

A statue of Austin Blair, governor of Michigan during the Civil War, stands in front of the state capitol in Lansing.

Michigan

Land & Water The Upper and Lower Peninsulas and Lakes Superior, Michigan, and Huron are important land and water features of Michigan.

Statehood Michigan became the 26th state in 1837.

People & Places Michigan's population is 10,003,422. Lansing is the state capital. The largest city is Detroit.

Fun Fact The record company Motown, named for Detroit's nickname "Motor City USA," grew from a small startup business in 1959 to one of the largest independent record companies in the world.

Boys explore nature's wonders on the bank of a river near Niles. The town sits on the site of Fort St. Joseph, built by the French in 1691.

▼ Snowmobiling is a popular winter sport on the Upper Peninsula. Michigan leads the U.S. in the number of registered snowmobiles. Many people also enjoy skiing and dog sledding.

Michigan State Flag

Apple Blossom State Flower

Robin State Bird

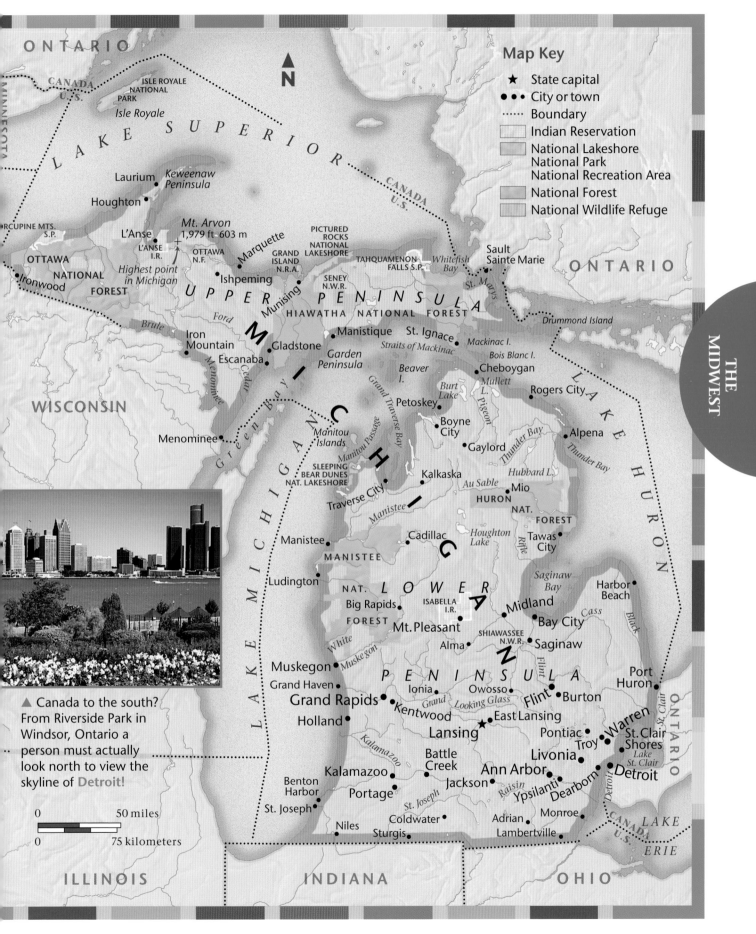

ONTARIO

CANADA
U.S.

ISLE ROYALE
NATIONAL
PARK

Isle Royale

N

LAKE SUPERIOR

CANADA
U.S.

Map Key

★ State capital
●●● City or town
⋯⋯ Boundary
Indian Reservation
National Lakeshore
National Park
National Recreation Area
National Forest
National Wildlife Refuge

MINNESOTA

Laurium
Keweenaw
Peninsula

Houghton

PORCUPINE MTS.
S.P.

OTTAWA
NATIONAL
FOREST

Ironwood

L'Anse
L'ANSE
I.R.

Mt. Arvon
1,979 ft 603 m

Highest point
in Michigan

OTTAWA
N.F.

Marquette

Ishpeming

Munising

GRAND
ISLAND
N.R.A.

PICTURED
ROCKS
NATIONAL
LAKESHORE

SENEY
N.W.R.

TAHQUAMENON
FALLS S.P.

Whitefish
Bay

Sault
Sainte Marie

St. Marys

ONTARIO

Drummond Island

UPPER   PENINSULA

HIAWATHA   NATIONAL   FOREST

Brule

Ford

MICHIGAN

Iron
Mountain

Gladstone

Escanaba

Menominee

Cedar

WISCONSIN

Menominee

Green Bay

Garden
Peninsula

Manistique

St. Ignace

Straits of Mackinac

Mackinac I.

Bois Blanc I.

Cheboygan

Beaver
I.

Burt
Lake

Mullett
L.

Pigeon

Rogers City

LAKE   HURON

Manitou
Islands

SLEEPING
BEAR DUNES
NAT. LAKESHORE

Manitou Passage

Grand Traverse Bay

Petoskey

Boyne
City

Gaylord

Thunder Bay

Alpena

Thunder Bay

Kalkaska

Au Sable

Hubbard L.

Mio

HURON

NAT.

FOREST

Traverse City

Manistee

Cadillac

Houghton
Lake

Rifle

Tawas
City

Manistee

MANISTEE

Ludington

NAT.

LOWER

Saginaw
Bay

Harbor
Beach

Big Rapids

ISABELLA
I.R.

Midland

Cass

FOREST

Mt. Pleasant

SHIAWASSEE
N.W.R.

Bay City

White

Muskegon

Muskegon

Alma

Saginaw

PENINSULA

Flint

Black

Grand Haven

Ionia

Owosso

Flint

Burton

Port
Huron

Grand Rapids

Kentwood

Grand

Looking Glass

St. Clair

ONTARIO

Holland

East Lansing

Pontiac

Troy

Warren

St. Clair
Shores

Lansing

Kalamazoo

Battle
Creek

Livonia

Lake
St. Clair

Kalamazoo

Ann Arbor

Dearborn

Detroit

Portage

Jackson

Ypsilanti

Detroit

Benton
Harbor

St. Joseph

St. Joseph

Coldwater

Raisin

Monroe

CANADA
U.S.

LAKE
ERIE

Niles

Sturgis

Adrian

Lambertville

▲ Canada to the south?
From Riverside Park in
Windsor, Ontario a
person must actually
look north to view the
skyline of Detroit!

0   50 miles

0   75 kilometers

ILLINOIS

INDIANA

OHIO

The Midwest

Minnesota

Land & Water Chippewa National Forest, Lake Superior, and the Mississippi River are important land and water features of Minnesota.

Statehood Minnesota became the 32nd state in 1858.

People & Places Minnesota's population is 5,220,393. St. Paul is the state capital. The largest city is Minneapolis.

Fun Fact Modern in-line skates were invented by two Minnesota students. Looking for a way to practice hockey in the summer, they replaced their skate blades with wheels.

◀ Minnesota's gray wolf population is growing and no longer endangered thanks to the work of the International Wolf Center in Ely.

▼ Some people in Minnesota sit for hours in "ice shacks" and fish through holes cut in the ice of frozen lakes.

Minnesota State Flag

Showy Lady's Slipper State Flower

Common Loon State Bird

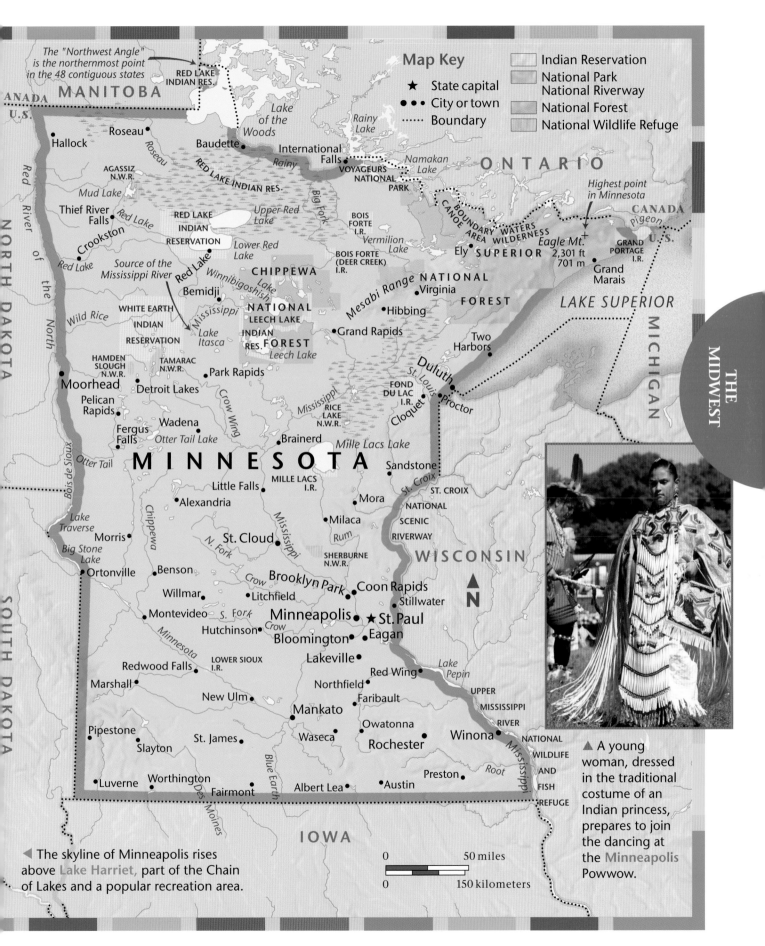

The "Northwest Angle" is the northernmost point in the 48 contiguous states

RED LAKE INDIAN RES.

CANADA
U.S.

MANITOBA

Hallock
Roseau
Baudette

Lake of the Woods

Rainy Lake

ONTARIO

Map Key

★ State capital
• • • City or town
•••••• Boundary

Indian Reservation
National Park
National Riverway
National Forest
National Wildlife Refuge

AGASSIZ N.W.R.
Mud Lake

Thief River Falls
Crookston
Red Lake

Roseau

RED LAKE INDIAN RES.

International Falls

Rainy

VOYAGEURS NATIONAL PARK

Namakan Lake

BOUNDARY WATERS

Highest point in Minnesota

CANADA
U.S.

Pigeon

RED LAKE INDIAN RESERVATION

Upper Red Lake

Lower Red Lake

Big Fork

BOIS FORTE I.R.

BOIS FORTE (DEER CREEK) I.R.

Vermilion Lake

CANOE AREA WILDERNESS

Ely

SUPERIOR

Eagle Mt.
2,301 ft
701 m

GRAND PORTAGE I.R.

Grand Marais

Source of the Mississippi River
Red Lake
Bemidji

Winnibigoshish

CHIPPEWA

NATIONAL

LEECH LAKE

Lake

Mesabi Range NATIONAL

Virginia
Hibbing

FOREST

LAKE SUPERIOR

MICHIGAN

WHITE EARTH INDIAN RESERVATION

Mississippi

Lake Itasca

INDIAN RES.

FOREST

Leech Lake

Grand Rapids

Two Harbors

Duluth

St. Louis

THE MIDWEST

HAMDEN SLOUGH N.W.R.
TAMARAC N.W.R.

Park Rapids

FOND DU LAC I.R.

Proctor

Moorhead
Detroit Lakes

Crow Wing

Mississippi

Cloquet

Pelican Rapids
Wadena

RICE LAKE N.W.R.

Wild Rice

Fergus Falls
Otter Tail Lake

Brainerd

Mille Lacs Lake

MINNESOTA

Sandstone

St. Croix

Otter Tail

Little Falls

MILLE LACS I.R.

ST. CROIX

Lake Traverse

Alexandria

Mora

NATIONAL

Big Stone Lake

Morris

Milaca

SCENIC

Ortonville

St. Cloud

Mississippi

Rum

RIVERWAY

SHERBURNE N.W.R.

WISCONSIN

Benson

N. Fork

Chippewa

Crow

Brooklyn Park

Coon Rapids

N

Willmar
Litchfield

Stillwater

Montevideo
S. Fork

Minneapolis
★ St. Paul

Hutchinson
Crow

Bloomington
Eagan

Redwood Falls

LOWER SIOUX I.R.

Lakeville

Minnesota

Red Wing

Lake Pepin

Marshall

Northfield

New Ulm

Faribault

UPPER

Mankato

Owatonna

MISSISSIPPI

Pipestone

St. James
Waseca

Rochester

Winona

RIVER

Slayton

Blue Earth

Preston

NATIONAL

Luverne
Worthington
Fairmont

Des Moines

Albert Lea

Austin

Root

Mississippi

WILDLIFE
AND
FISH
REFUGE

IOWA

NORTH DAKOTA

Red River of the North

SOUTH DAKOTA

Bois de Sioux

◀ The skyline of Minneapolis rises above Lake Harriet, part of the Chain of Lakes and a popular recreation area.

0   50 miles

0   150 kilometers

▲ A young woman, dressed in the traditional costume of an Indian princess, prepares to join the dancing at the Minneapolis Powwow.

Missouri

Land & Water

Mark Twain National Forest and the Missouri and Mississippi Rivers are important land and water features of Missouri.

Statehood
Missouri became the 24th state in 1821.

People & Places

Missouri's population is 5,911,605. Jefferson City is the state capital. The largest city is Kansas City.

Fun Fact
Mark Twain's childhood in Hannibal, a town on the Mississippi River, inspired many of his books, including *The Adventures of Tom Sawyer* and *The Adventures of Huckleberry Finn.*

Missouri State Flag

**Eastern Bluebird
State Bird**

**Hawthorn
State Flower**

▲ In 1804, the Lewis and Clark Expedition set off from St. Charles, Missouri, to explore the Northwest Territories. In 2004 the bicentennial of this important event was celebrated.

◄ Gateway Arch, completed in 1965, recognizes the role played by St. Louis in U.S. westward expansion. Trams carry one million tourists to the top of the arch each year.

IOWA

NEBR.

Missouri

Maryville

Bethany

Thompson

Grand

Trenton

Kirksville

Locust Creek

Chariton

Brookfield

Chillicothe

Middle Fabius

South Fabius

Wyaconda

Mississippi

SWAN LAKE
N.W.R.

Hannibal

Salt

0   50 miles
0   75 kilometers

N

Map Key

★ State capital
••• City or town
······ Boundary
National Riverway
National Forest
National Wildlife
Refuge

St. Joseph

Platte

Liberty

Richmond

Kansas City

Independence

Blue Springs

Lees Summit

Warrensburg

Blackwater

Marshall

Boonville

Sedalia

Moberly

Mexico

Columbia

MARK TWAIN
NATIONAL
FOREST

Fulton

Mark Twain
Lake

CLARENCE
CANNON
N.W.R.

Cuivre

St. Charles

St. Peters

Florissant

Ferguson

University City

St. Louis

ILLINOIS

KANSAS

South Grand

Harry S. Truman
Reservoir

Osage

Jefferson City ★

Missouri

Washington

Kirkwood

Mississippi

MISSOURI

Osage

Nevada

Sac

Stockton
Lake

Bolivar

Niangua

Osage Fork

Lake of
the Ozarks

Gasconade

Rolla

Sullivan

De Soto

MARK TWAIN

Salem

NATIONAL

FOREST

Highest point
in Missouri

Taum Sauk Mt.
1,772 ft 540 m

Farmington

Jackson

Cape Girardeau

Ohio

KENTUCKY

Lebanon

Little Sac

Carthage

Springfield

Joplin

Neosho

Ava

Gasconade

Bryant Creek

Big Piney

OZARK
NATIONAL
SCENIC RIVERWAYS

Current

PLATEAU

Eleven Point

West Plains

MINGO
N.W.R.

Sikeston

Poplar Bluff

Black

Mississippi

TENNESSEE

Table Rock Lake

MARK TWAIN NATIONAL FOREST

O Z A R K

Branson

White

Bull Shoals Lake

OKLAHOMA

ARKANSAS

Kennett

◀ A cannon stands
as a silent reminder
of battles fought in
Missouri during the
Civil War. Missouri
was a border state that
gave support to both
sides during the war.

◀ White-tailed deer live
throughout Missouri,
but are most abundant in
the Missouri River hills.

North Dakota

▲ North Dakota's sedimentary rocks offered ideal conditions for formation of fossils such as this leaf.

Land & Water The Great Plains, the Badlands, and the Missouri River are important land and water features of North Dakota.

Statehood North Dakota became the 39th state in 1889.

People & Places North Dakota's population is 641,481. Bismarck is the state capital. The largest city is Fargo.

Fun Fact North Dakota leads the country in production of sunflower seeds—more than a billion pounds each year. Sunflowers grow as tall as 13 feet (4 m).

▲ Cowboys on the fence watch the excitement of the rodeo during the Slope County Fair in Amidon.

CANADA
U.S.
SASKATCH

Crosby •

MONTANA

Little Muddy

Tioga •

Williston

Missouri

LITTL

Watford City •

THEODORE ROOSEVELT N.P. (NORTH UNIT)

Little Miss

MISSOURI

THEODORE ROOSEVELT N.P. (ELKHORN RANCH SITE)

Yellowstone

Badlands

NATIONAL

THEODORE ROOSEVELT N. (SOUTH UNIT)

Medora

Dickinson

GRASSLAND

Amidon

+ White Butt 3,506 ft 1,069 m ◄

Little Missouri

• Bowman

Ce

Hettin

0   100 miles
0   150 kilometer

N

North Dakota State Flag

Wild Prairie Rose
State Flower

Western
Meadowlark
State Bird

◄ American bison are native to the Great Plains, but now are found mainly in parks such as Sullys Hill National Game Preserve in North Dakota.

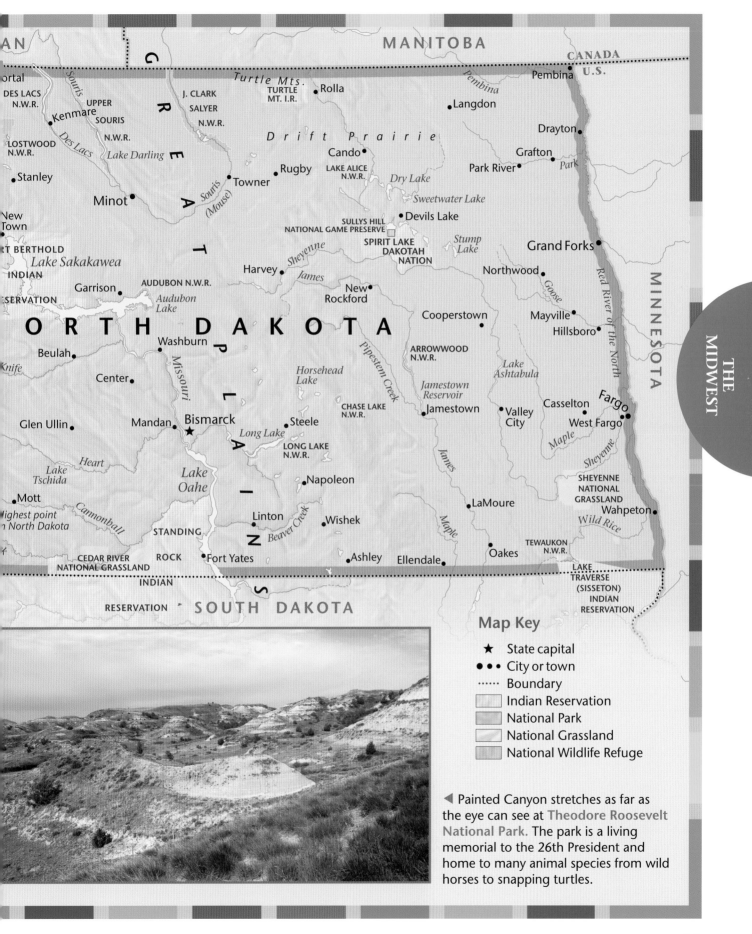

MANITOBA

CANADA
U.S.

AN

GREAT

ortal

DES LACS
N.W.R.

Souris

Kenmare

UPPER
SOURIS
N.W.R.

Des Lacs

LOSTWOOD
N.W.R.

Lake Darling

Stanley

Minot

New
Town

RT BERTHOLD

Lake Sakakawea

INDIAN

RESERVATION

Garrison

Audubon
Lake

Turtle Mts.

Rolla

TURTLE
MT. I.R.

J. CLARK
SALYER
N.W.R.

Drift Prairie

Cando

Rugby

LAKE ALICE
N.W.R.

Dry Lake

Towner

Souris
(Mouse)

Sweetwater Lake

SULLYS HILL
NATIONAL GAME PRESERVE

Devils Lake

SPIRIT LAKE
DAKOTAH
NATION

Stump
Lake

Harvey

Sheyenne

James

New
Rockford

AUDUBON N.W.R.

Langdon

Drayton

Grafton

Park River

Park

Grand Forks

Northwood

Goose

Cooperstown

Mayville

Hillsboro

MINNESOTA

Pembina

Pembina

ORTH DAKOTA

PLAINS

Beulah

Knife

Center

Washburn

Missouri

Glen Ullin

Mandan

Bismarck ★

Lake
Tschida

Heart

Mott

Lake
Oahe

Horsehead
Lake

Steele

Long Lake

LONG LAKE
N.W.R.

Napoleon

Pipestem Creek

CHASE LAKE
N.W.R.

ARROWWOOD
N.W.R.

Jamestown
Reservoir

Jamestown

Lake
Ashtabula

Valley
City

Casselton

West Fargo

Maple

Fargo

Sheyenne

SHEYENNE
NATIONAL
GRASSLAND

Wahpeton

Highest point
n North Dakota

Cannonball

STANDING

Linton

Beaver Creek

Wishek

James

LaMoure

Maple

Wild Rice

CEDAR RIVER
NATIONAL GRASSLAND

ROCK

Fort Yates

Ashley

Ellendale

Oakes

TEWAUKON
N.W.R.

LAKE
TRAVERSE
(SISSETON)
INDIAN
RESERVATION

INDIAN

RESERVATION

SOUTH DAKOTA

Red River of the North

Map Key

★ State capital
••• City or town
...... Boundary
▨ Indian Reservation
▨ National Park
▨ National Grassland
▨ National Wildlife Refuge

◀ Painted Canyon stretches as far as
the eye can see at Theodore Roosevelt
National Park. The park is a living
memorial to the 26th President and
home to many animal species from wild
horses to snapping turtles.

The Midwest

Ohio

 Land & Water Wayne National Forest, Lake Erie, and the Ohio River are important land and water features of Ohio.

 Statehood Ohio became the 17th state in 1803.

People & Places Ohio's population is 11,485,910. Columbus is the state capital and the largest city.

Fun Fact Ohio's nickname, the Buckeye State, comes from a local tree. The tree's common name was derived from the Native Americans, who thought its seeds looked like the eye of a male deer, or buck.

▲ Fourth of July fireworks light up the night-time sky above **Columbus**. The city has been the state capital since 1816.

▲ Colorful guitars mark the entrance to the Rock and Roll Hall of Fame, established in downtown **Cleveland** in 1995.

▼ The Blue Streak is the oldest operating roller coaster at Cedar Point Amusement Park in **Sandusky**. This popular ride is named after a local high school sports team.

Ohio State Flag

Scarlet Carnation State Flower

Cardinal State Bird

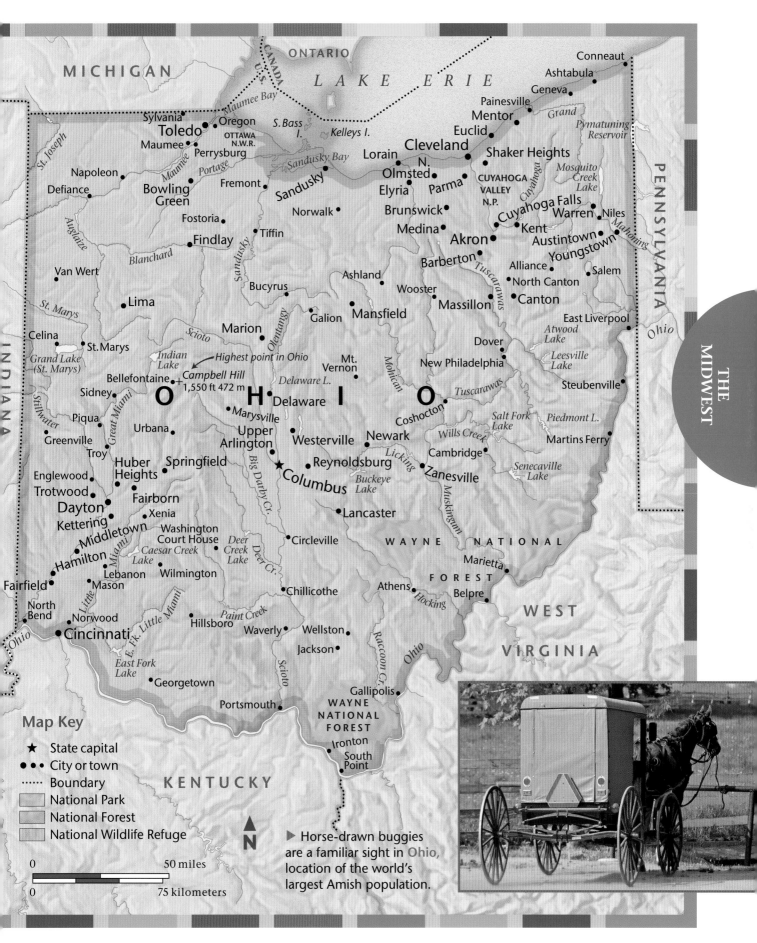

MICHIGAN

ONTARIO

CANADA
U.S.

LAKE ERIE

Conneaut
Ashtabula
Geneva
Painesville
Mentor
Grand
Pymatuning
Reservoir

Sylvania
Oregon
Toledo
Maumee
Perrysburg
OTTAWA
N.W.R.
S. Bass I.
Kelleys I.
Maumee Bay

Euclid
Cleveland
Shaker Heights
Lorain
N.
Olmsted
Mosquito
Creek
Lake
Cuyahoga

Napoleon
Bowling Green
Defiance
Fremont
Sandusky
Sandusky Bay
Norwalk
Elyria
Parma
Brunswick
Medina
CUYAHOGA VALLEY N.P.
Cuyahoga Falls
Warren
Niles
Kent
Austintown
Youngstown
Mahoning

St. Joseph
Auglaize
Portage
Blanchard
Fostoria
Findlay
Tiffin
Bucyrus
Ashland
Wooster
Akron
Barberton
Massillon
Alliance
North Canton
Canton
Salem

Van Wert
Lima
Marion
Galion
Mansfield
East Liverpool
Atwood Lake
Leesville Lake

Celina
St. Marys
St. Marys
Grand Lake
(St. Marys)
Scioto
Olentangy
Indian Lake
Bellefontaine
Highest point in Ohio
Campbell Hill
1,550 ft 472 m
Mt. Vernon
Delaware L.
Delaware
Dover
New Philadelphia
Tuscarawas
Coshocton
Salt Fork Lake
Steubenville
Piedmont L.
Martins Ferry

O   H   I   O

Sidney
Piqua
Urbana
Marysville
Upper Arlington
Westerville
Newark
Cambridge
Senecaville Lake

Greenville
Troy
Huber Heights
Springfield
Reynoldsburg
Columbus
Licking
Wills Creek
Zanesville

Englewood
Trotwood
Dayton
Fairborn
Xenia
Buckeye Lake
Lancaster
Muskingum

Kettering
Middletown
Washington Court House
Circleville
WAYNE   NATIONAL   FOREST

Hamilton
Caesar Creek Lake
Deer Creek Lake
Deer Cr.
Marietta

Fairfield
Lebanon
Mason
Wilmington
Chillicothe
Athens
Hocking
Belpre

North Bend
Norwood
Cincinnati
Hillsboro
Paint Creek
Waverly
Wellston
Jackson
Raccoon Cr.
Ohio

WEST

VIRGINIA

Georgetown
Portsmouth
Scioto
Gallipolis
WAYNE NATIONAL FOREST
Ironton
South Point

St. Marys
Stillwater
Great Miami
Miami
Little Miami
E. Fk. Little Miami
East Fork Lake

INDIANA

PENNSYLVANIA
Ohio

Map Key

★ State capital
●●● City or town
⋯⋯ Boundary
National Park
National Forest
National Wildlife Refuge

0   50 miles
0   75 kilometers

N

KENTUCKY

▶ Horse-drawn buggies are a familiar sight in Ohio, location of the world's largest Amish population.

The Midwest

South Dakota

▲ A mountain cottontail nibbles on some grass in Wind Cave National Park.

Land & Water The Black Hills, National Grasslands, and the Missouri River are important land and water features of South Dakota.

Statehood South Dakota became the 40th state in 1889.

People & Places South Dakota's population is 804,194. Pierre is the state capital. The largest city is Sioux Falls.

Fun Fact The world's largest, most complete, and best preserved specimen of *Tyrannosaurus rex,* nicknamed Sue, was unearthed on the Cheyenne River Sioux Indian Reservation in 1990.

BEWARE
TYRANNOSAURUS
AHEAD

◀ A funny sign warns South Dakota motorists of a dinosaur crossing.

MONTANA

CUSTER
NATIONAL
FOREST

Little Missouri

Buffalo

North Fork

South Fork

Sulphur C

GRA
R
S. Fork Gra

•Belle Fourche

•Spearfish

Lead• •Deadwood •Sturgis

BLACK

Black Hills

Belle Fourc

WYOMING

HILLS

Rapid City

•Highest poin in South Dak

CRAZY HORSE MEMORIAL

MOUNT RUSHMORE N

Harney Peak
7,242 ft 2,207 m

NATIONAL CUSTER S.P.

Hot Springs

WIND CAVE N.P.

Cheyenne

FOREST

•Edgemont

GAP

PA

P

INDI

BUFFALO

White

Pir Ridg

0   50 miles
0   75 kilometers

N

▼ Carvings on Mount Rushmore in the Black Hills honor four past presidents (from left to right): George Washington, Thomas Jefferson, Theodore Roosevelt, and Abraham Lincoln.

South Dakota State Flag

Pasqueflower
State Flower

Ring-Necked Pheasant
State Bird

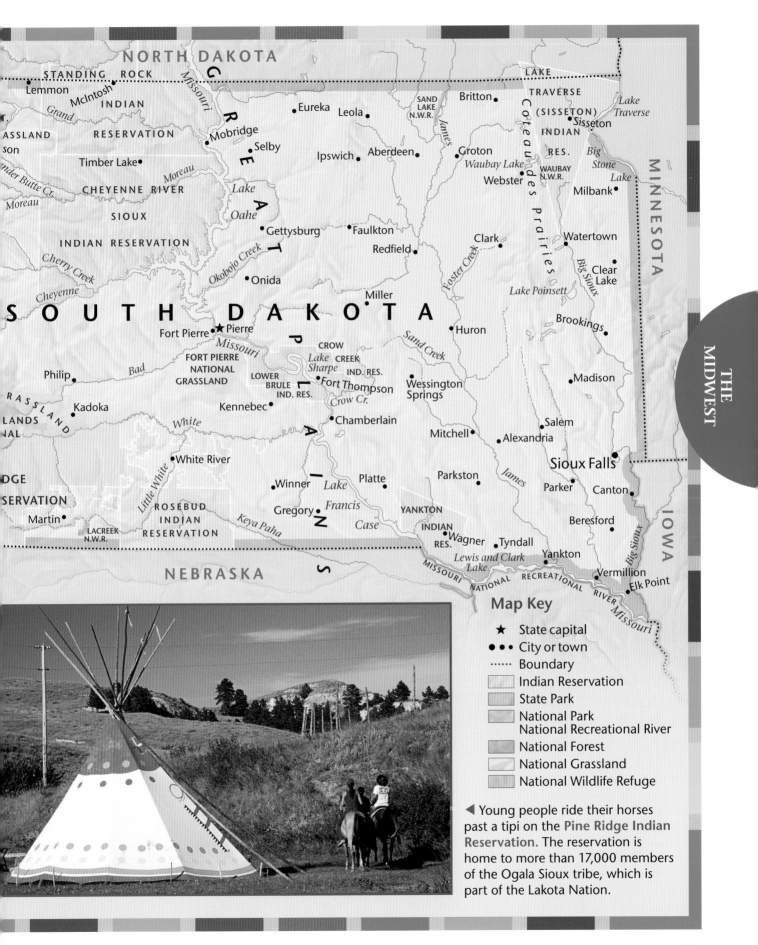

NORTH DAKOTA

STANDING ROCK

Lemmon
McIntosh
INDIAN
RESERVATION
son
GRASSLAND
Grand
Moreau
der Butte Cr.
Moreau
Timber Lake
CHEYENNE RIVER
SIOUX
INDIAN RESERVATION
Cherry Creek
Cheyenne

Missouri
Mobridge
Selby
Lake Oahe
Gettysburg
Okobojo Creek
Onida

Eureka
Leola
Ipswich
Aberdeen

SAND
LAKE
N.W.R.

Britton

Groton
Waubay Lake
Webster

James

LAKE
TRAVERSE
(SISSETON)
INDIAN
RES.

Lake
Traverse
Sisseton

WAUBAY
N.W.R.

Big
Stone
Lake

Milbank

MINNESOTA

Faulkton
Redfield

Clark

Foster Creek

Watertown

Lake Poinsett

Clear
Lake

Big Sioux

SOUTH DAKOTA

Miller

Huron

Brookings

Fort Pierre ★ Pierre
Missouri
Bad
FORT PIERRE
NATIONAL
GRASSLAND

Philip

RASSLAND

LANDS
AL

Kadoka

LOWER
BRULE
IND. RES.

Lake
Sharpe

CROW
CREEK
IND. RES.
Fort Thompson
Crow Cr.

Sand Creek

Wessington
Springs

Madison

Kennebec

White

Chamberlain

Mitchell
Alexandria

Salem

Parkston

DGE

White River

SERVATION

Martin

LACREEK
N.W.R.

Little White

ROSEBUD
INDIAN
RESERVATION

Winner

Keya Paha

Gregory

Lake
Francis

Platte

Case

YANKTON
INDIAN
RES.

James

Parker

Sioux Falls

Canton

Beresford

Big Sioux

IOWA

Wagner
Tyndall

Lewis and Clark
Lake

Yankton

Vermillion
Elk Point

NEBRASKA

MISSOURI
NATIONAL
RECREATIONAL
RIVER
Missouri

Map Key

★ State capital
••• City or town
······ Boundary
Indian Reservation
State Park
National Park
National Recreational River
National Forest
National Grassland
National Wildlife Refuge

◀ Young people ride their horses past a tipi on the **Pine Ridge Indian Reservation**. The reservation is home to more than 17,000 members of the Ogala Sioux tribe, which is part of the Lakota Nation.

Wisconsin

Land & Water Apostle Islands, Green Bay, and Lakes Superior and Michigan are important land and water features of Wisconsin.

Statehood
Wisconsin became the 30th state in 1848.

People & Places
Wisconsin's population is 5,627,967. Madison is the state capital. The largest city is Milwaukee.

Fun Fact Laura Ingalls Wilder was born in Pepin in 1867. Her famous "Little House" books are based on her childhood in the forests and prairies of the Midwest.

▲ In Wisconsin the bald eagle is found only in the northern regions.

◀ A young Native American man dressed in colorful traditional costume dances at a festival in Milwaukee.

▲ In a winter version of sailing, ice boats compete in a race on the frozen surface of Lake Winnebago near Oshkosh.

WISCONSIN

1848

Wisconsin State Flag

Robin
State Bird

Wood Violet
State Flower

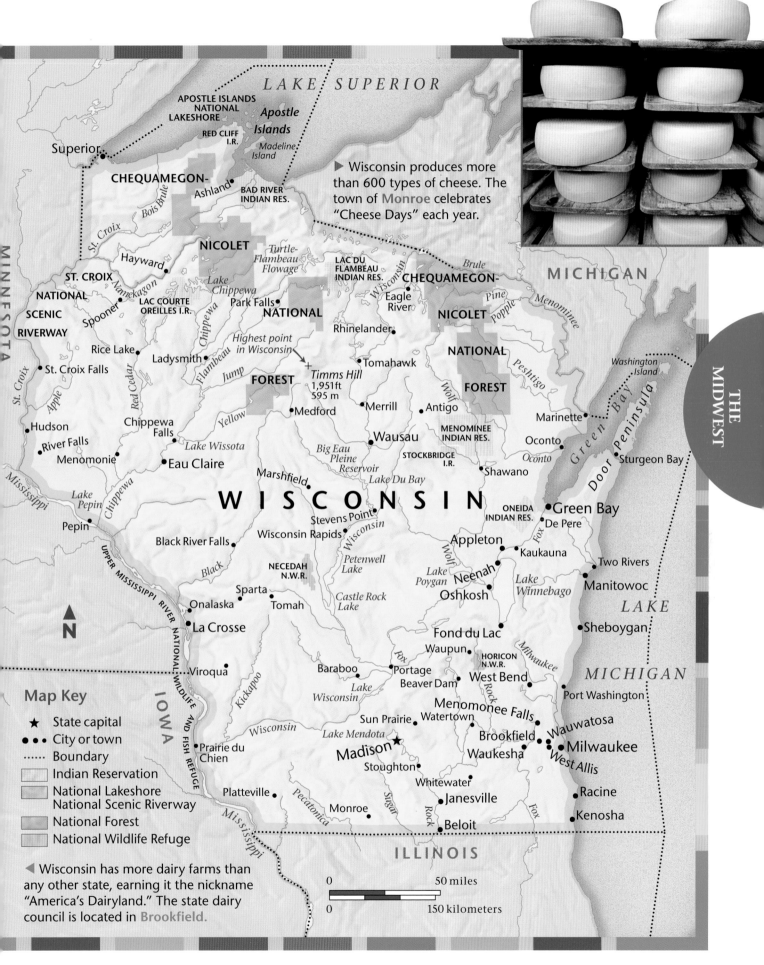

▶ Wisconsin produces more than 600 types of cheese. The town of Monroe celebrates "Cheese Days" each year.

◀ Wisconsin has more dairy farms than any other state, earning it the nickname "America's Dairyland." The state dairy council is located in Brookfield.

THE MIDWEST

The Southwest

The Southwest region extends from the humid Gulf Coast in the east to the arid canyonlands in the west. The people of the region are just as varied as the natural landscape. Native Americans, descendants of early Spanish settlers, and recent immigrants from Mexico and Central America contribute to this region's special cultural landscape. Agriculture, cattle ranching, and the oil industry are traditional economic activities. The Southwest is a part of the Sunbelt where rapid population growth and sprawling cities are putting pressure on the region's limited water resources.

A rainbow frames Cerro Castellon in Big Bend National Park. This eroded mount of volcanic rock rises almost 3,300 feet (1,006 m) above the desert floor. Raising horses is a part of the cultural tradition in this region.

The Southwest

Arizona

Land & Water
The Colorado Plateau, the Grand Canyon, and the Colorado River are important land and water features of Arizona.

Statehood
Arizona became the 48th state in 1912.

People & Places
Arizona's population is 6,500,180. Phoenix is the state capital and the largest city.

Fun Fact
Of the 21 Indian reservations in Arizona, the largest belongs to the Navajo Nation. Native peoples and the federal government own 70 percent of the state.

▲ Daring boaters get soaked as they run the rapids on the fast flowing waters of the **Colorado River** in Grand Canyon National Park.

► Saguaro cacti, found in the **Sonoran Desert**, can grow to more than 30 feet (9 m).

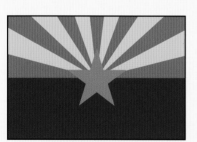

Arizona State Flag

Cactus Wren
State Bird

Saguaro
State Flower

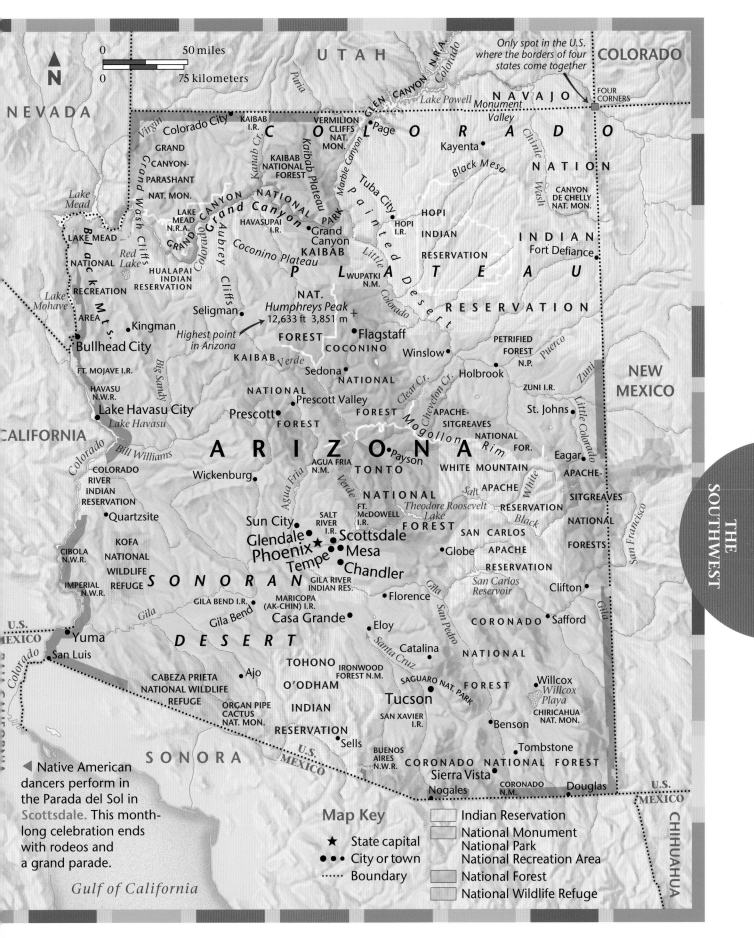

N

0 ——— 50 miles
0 ——— 75 kilometers

NEVADA

UTAH

COLORADO

Only spot in the U.S. where the borders of four states come together

GLEN CANYON N.R.A.

Lake Powell

Monument Valley

NAVAJO

FOUR CORNERS

Colorado City

KAIBAB I.R.

VERMILION CLIFFS NAT. MON.

Page

Kayenta

Black Mesa

Chinle Wash

COLORADO

NATION

CANYON DE CHELLY NAT. MON.

GRAND CANYON-PARASHANT NAT. MON.

KAIBAB NATIONAL FOREST

Kaibab Plateau

Marble Canyon

Tuba City

HOPI I.R.

HOPI INDIAN RESERVATION

INDIAN

Fort Defiance

Lake Mead

LAKE MEAD N.R.A.

GRAND CANYON NATIONAL PARK

Grand Canyon

Painted Desert

GRAND

HAVASUPAI I.R.

KAIBAB

LAKE MEAD NATIONAL RECREATION AREA

Black Mts.

Red Lake

HUALAPAI INDIAN RESERVATION

Coconino Plateau

COLORADO PLATEAU

WUPATKI N.M.

RESERVATION

Lake Mohave

Kingman

Seligman

NAT. FOREST

Humphreys Peak 12,633 ft 3,851 m

Highest point in Arizona

Flagstaff

COCONINO

Winslow

PETRIFIED FOREST N.P.

Puerco

NEW MEXICO

Bullhead City

FT. MOJAVE I.R.

KAIBAB

Verde

Sedona

NATIONAL

Holbrook

Clear Cr.

ZUNI I.R.

Zuni

HAVASU N.W.R.

Big Sandy

NATIONAL

Prescott Valley

FOREST

Chevelon Cr.

APACHE-SITGREAVES

St. Johns

Little Colorado

Lake Havasu City

Lake Havasu

Prescott

FOREST

Mogollon Rim

NATIONAL FOR.

Eagar

CALIFORNIA

Colorado

Bill Williams

ARIZONA

AGUA FRIA N.M.

Payson

WHITE MOUNTAIN

APACHE-SITGREAVES

Wickenburg

Agua Fria

TONTO

APACHE

Salt

NATIONAL

COLORADO RIVER INDIAN RESERVATION

Verde

NATIONAL

FT. McDOWELL I.R.

Theodore Roosevelt Lake

Black

White

RESERVATION

FORESTS

San Francisco

Quartzsite

Sun City

SALT RIVER I.R.

FOREST

SAN CARLOS

KOFA NATIONAL WILDLIFE REFUGE

Glendale

Scottsdale

Globe

APACHE

CIBOLA N.W.R.

Phoenix

Mesa

RESERVATION

SONORAN

Tempe

Chandler

IMPERIAL N.W.R.

GILA RIVER INDIAN RES.

San Carlos Reservoir

Clifton

Gila

Florence

CORONADO

Safford

Gila

MARICOPA (AK-CHIN) I.R.

Eloy

San Pedro

NATIONAL

Yuma

GILA BEND I.R.

Gila Bend

Casa Grande

Catalina

Santa Cruz

U.S. MEXICO

San Luis

DESERT

CABEZA PRIETA NATIONAL WILDLIFE REFUGE

Ajo

TOHONO

IRONWOOD FOREST N.M.

O'ODHAM

SAGUARO NAT. PARK

FOREST

Willcox

Willcox Playa

Colorado

ORGAN PIPE CACTUS NAT. MON.

INDIAN

Tucson

CHIRICAHUA NAT. MON.

SAN XAVIER I.R.

Benson

RESERVATION

Sells

BUENOS AIRES N.W.R.

Tombstone

SONORA

U.S. MEXICO

CORONADO NATIONAL FOREST

Sierra Vista

Nogales

CORONADO N.M.

Douglas

U.S. MEXICO

CHIHUAHUA

◀ Native American dancers perform in the Parada del Sol in Scottsdale. This month-long celebration ends with rodeos and a grand parade.

Gulf of California

Map Key

★ State capital
••• City or town
••••• Boundary

Indian Reservation
National Monument
National Park
National Recreation Area
National Forest
National Wildlife Refuge

THE SOUTHWEST

New Mexico

 Land & Water The Sangre de Cristo Mountains, Carlsbad Caverns, and the Rio Grande are important land and water features of New Mexico.

Statehood New Mexico became the 47th state in 1912.

People & Places New Mexico's population is 1,984,356. Santa Fe is the state capital. The largest city is Albuquerque.

Fun Fact Roswell is a popular destination for people interested in UFOs. A local rancher discovered what he believed to be wreckage of a UFO in 1947.

▲ Brightly colored balloons rise into a blue sky in **Albuquerque** during the International Balloon Fiesta, the largest such event in the world.

◀ The caves of **Carlsbad Caverns** were created as natural sulfuric acid dissolved the limestone rocks.

▼ Chili peppers, seen here in a store in **Santa Fe**, give Southwestern food a distinctive taste. New Mexico is the leading U.S. producer of chilies.

New Mexico State Flag

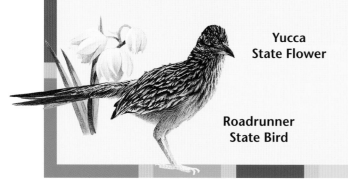

**Yucca
State Flower**

**Roadrunner
State Bird**

Only spot in the U.S. where the borders of four states come together

FOUR CORNERS

COLORADO

UT.

VAJO

NATION

INDIAN

RESERVATION

ATION

OR.

UTE MOUNTAIN I. R.

San Juan

Shiprock

Aztec

Farmington

Bloomfield

Navajo Reservoir

CARSON NATIONAL FOREST

JICARILLA APACHE

INDIAN

RESERVATION

Cañon Largo

Navajo

Crownpoint

Gallup

Zuni

ZUNI INDIAN RES.

RAMAH NAVAJO IND. RES.

CHACO CULTURE N.H.P.

Milan

Grants

EL MALPAIS N.M.

TO'HAJIILEE NAVAJO

CIBOLA NATIONAL FOREST

Continental Divide

San Juan

Chama

ROCKY

CARSON

Wheeler Peak 13,161 ft 4,011 m

NATIONAL

Taos

TAOS I.R.

FOREST

Chimayo

SANTE FE

SANTA CLARA I.R.

Los Alamos

NAT.

BANDELIER N.M.

COCHITI I.R.

NAMBE I.R.

Rio Grande

Sangre de Cristo Mts.

Highest point in New Mexico

Springer

Pecos Baldy Lake

★ Santa Fe

FOREST

Las Vegas

LAS VEGAS N.W.R.

Raton

MAXWELL N.W.R.

Dry Cimarron

Corrumpa Creek

Carrizo Creek

Clayton

KIOWA AND RITA BLANCA NATIONAL GRASSLANDS

OKLA.

Mora

Ute Creek

Canadian

JEMEZ IND. RES.

ZIA IND. RES.

SANTO DOMINGO I.R.

SANTA ANA I.R.

SAN FELIPE I.R.

SANDIA I.R.

LAGUNA I.R.

Bernalillo

Rio San José

LAGUNA

ACOMA I.R.

INDIAN

RESERVATION

ISLETA IND. RES.

Rio Puerco

Rio Rancho

Albuquerque

CIBOLA

Los Lunas

Belen

NATIONAL

ALAMO NAVAJO I.R.

SEVILLETA N.W.R.

Moriarty

Estancia

Mountainair

FOREST

Conchas Lake

Conchas

Santa Rosa Lake

Gallinas

Pecos

Santa Rosa

Tucumcari

Sumner Lake

Fort Sumner

Clovis

Portales

N E W   M E X I C O

CIBOLA

Socorro

NATIONAL

FOREST

Rio Grande

San Andres Mountains

Gallo Arroyo

Arroyo del Macho

Sacramento

Pecos

LLANO

ESTACADO

THE SOUTHWEST

APACHE-

GREAVES

TIONAL

Reserve

GILA

NATIONAL

FOREST

Bayard

Silver City

San Francisco

Gila

Lordsburg

Deming

Continental Divide

BOSQUE DEL APACHE N.W.R.

Black Range

Truth or Consequences

Elephant Butte Res.

Caballo Reservoir

Las Cruces

Carrizozo

LINCOLN

Tularosa

MESCALERO APACHE INDIAN RES.

Alamogordo

WHITE SANDS N.M.

SAN ANDRES N.W.R.

Mountains

Sacramento Mountains

NATIONAL

BITTER LAKE N.W.R.

Roswell

Rio Hondo

Hagerman

Artesia

Rio Peñasco

FOREST

Guadalupe Mts.

Loving

CARLSBAD CAVERNS N.P.

Carlsbad

Brantley Lake

Pecos

Lovington

Hobbs

Eunice

TEXAS

Anthony

Sunland Park

Rio Grande

U.S. MEXICO

CORONADO NATIONAL FOREST

U.S. MEXICO

CHIHUAHUA

U.S. MEXICO

N

Map Key

★ State capital

••• City or town

······ Boundary

Indian Reservation

National Monument National Park

National Forest

National Wildlife Refuge

0   50 miles

0   75 kilometers

Oklahoma

Land & Water Black Mesa, the Wichita Mountains, and the Arkansas River are important land and water features of Oklahoma.

Statehood Oklahoma became the 46th state in 1907.

People & Places Oklahoma's population is 3,642,361. Oklahoma City is the state capital and the largest city.

Fun Fact Before it became a state, Oklahoma was known as Indian Territory. Today 39 Indian nations, including Cherokees, Osages, Creeks, and Choctaws, have their headquarters in the state.

▲ A tornado is a destructive rotating column of air that forms from a thunderstorm. In 1974, five tornadoes struck Oklahoma City in one day.

Oklahoma State Flag

OKLAHOMA

Mistletoe State Flower

Scissor-Tailed Flycatcher State Bird

▲ The Golden Driller, with his hand on an oil rig, stands 76 feet (23 m) tall near the State Fairgrounds in Tulsa.

COLORADO

Cimarron

Black Mesa
4,973 ft
1,516 m • Boise City **H I G H** Beaver
Highest point • Guymon Beaver •
in Oklahoma

NEW MEXICO

KIOWA AND
RITA BLANCA
NAT. GRASSLAND **P L A I N S**

Optima Lake

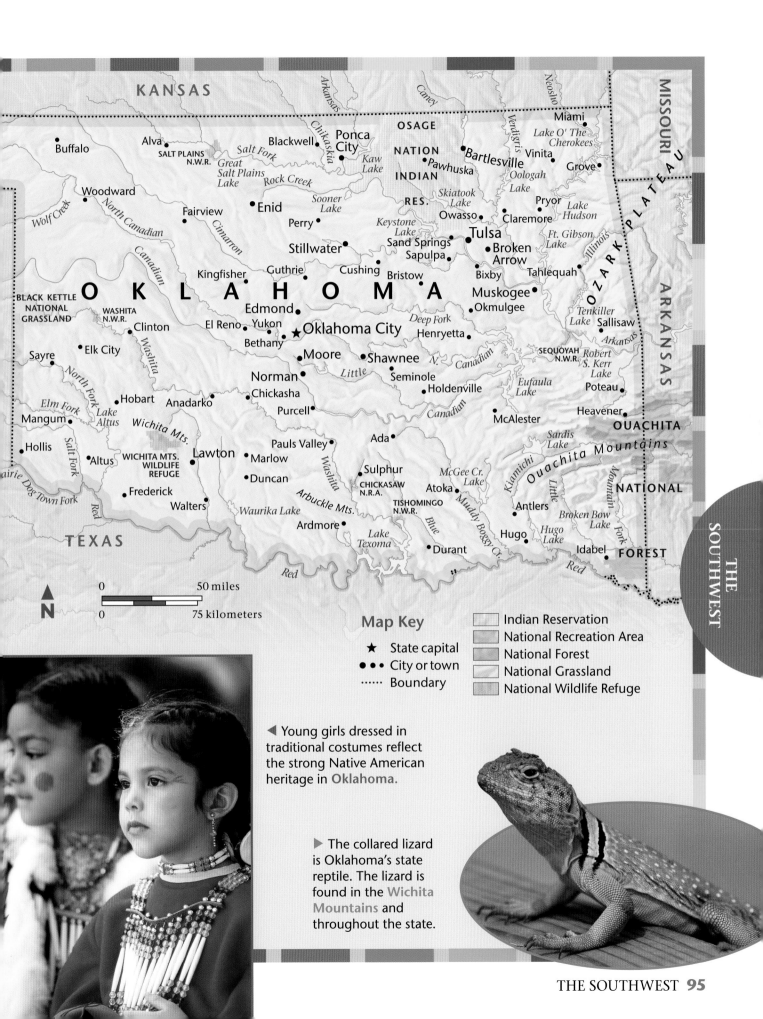

KANSAS

MISSOURI

Buffalo

Alva

Blackwell

Chikaskia

Arkansas

Caney

Neosho

Ponca City

OSAGE

Miami

Lake O' The Cherokees

Salt Fork

SALT PLAINS N.W.R.

Great Salt Plains Lake

Kaw Lake

NATION

Bartlesville

Vinita

Rock Creek

INDIAN

Pawhuska

Grove

Woodward

North Canadian

Sooner Lake

RES.

Skiatook Lake

Oologah Lake

Pryor

Lake Hudson

Wolf Creek

Fairview

Enid

Perry

Owasso

Claremore

Cimarron

Keystone Lake

Tulsa

Ft. Gibson Lake

OZARK

ARKANSAS

Stillwater

Sand Springs

Broken Arrow

BLACK KETTLE NATIONAL GRASSLAND

O K L A H O M A

Kingfisher

Guthrie

Cushing

Bristow

Sapulpa

Bixby

Tahlequah

PLATEAU

WASHITA N.W.R.

Clinton

El Reno

Yukon

Edmond

Muskogee

Okmulgee

Tenkiller Lake

Sallisaw

Arkansas

Washita

★ Oklahoma City

Deep Fork

Bethany

Sayre

Elk City

Moore

Shawnee

Henryetta

SEQUOYAH N.W.R.

Robert S. Kerr Lake

North Fork

Hobart

Anadarko

Norman

N. Canadian

Seminole

Eufaula Lake

Poteau

Elm Fork

Lake Altus

Chickasha

Little

Holdenville

Mangum

Purcell

Canadian

Heavener

Hollis

Salt Fork

Altus

WICHITA MTS. WILDLIFE REFUGE

Lawton

Pauls Valley

Ada

McAlester

OUACHITA

airie Dog Town Fork

Frederick

Marlow

Washita

Sardis Lake

Ouachita Mountains

Duncan

Sulphur

McGee Cr. Lake

Kiamichi

NATIONAL

Walters

CHICKASAW N.R.A.

Atoka

Little

Mountain

TEXAS

Waurika Lake

TISHOMINGO N.W.R.

Antlers

Broken Bow Lake

Red

Ardmore

Lake Texoma

Blue

Muddy Boggy Cr.

Hugo

Hugo Lake

Fork

FOREST

Durant

Idabel

Red

Red

0   50 miles

N

0   75 kilometers

Map Key

★ State capital

●●● City or town

⋯⋯ Boundary

☐ Indian Reservation

☐ National Recreation Area

☐ National Forest

☐ National Grassland

☐ National Wildlife Refuge

◀ Young girls dressed in traditional costumes reflect the strong Native American heritage in Oklahoma.

▶ The collared lizard is Oklahoma's state reptile. The lizard is found in the Wichita Mountains and throughout the state.

The Southwest

Texas

▲ The brightly lit Congress Avenue Bridge crosses the Town Lake, leading into downtown Austin where tall buildings rise against the night sky.

 Land & Water The Edwards Plateau, Padre Island National Seashore, and the Rio Grande are important land and water features of Texas.

Statehood Texas became the 28th state in 1845.

People & Places The population of Texas is 24,326,974. Austin is the state capital. The largest city is Houston.

Fun Fact Over the course of its history, six different national flags have flown over Texas—Spanish, French, Mexican, Texan, Confederate, and American.

NEW MEXICO

GUADALUPE MTS. N.P.

U.S.
MEXICO
El Paso
Guadalupe Peak
8,749 ft
2,667 m
Highest point in Texas

CHIHUAHUA

Rio Grande

Davis M

Marfa

Presid

◄ Texas leads the U.S. in oil and natural gas production. A well near Houston pumps oil, called "black gold" because it's worth so much money.

Texas State Flag

Mockingbird State Bird

Bluebonnet State Flower

▼ The colorful coach whip snake is found in west Texas. It can grow up to 6 feet (1.8 m) in length.

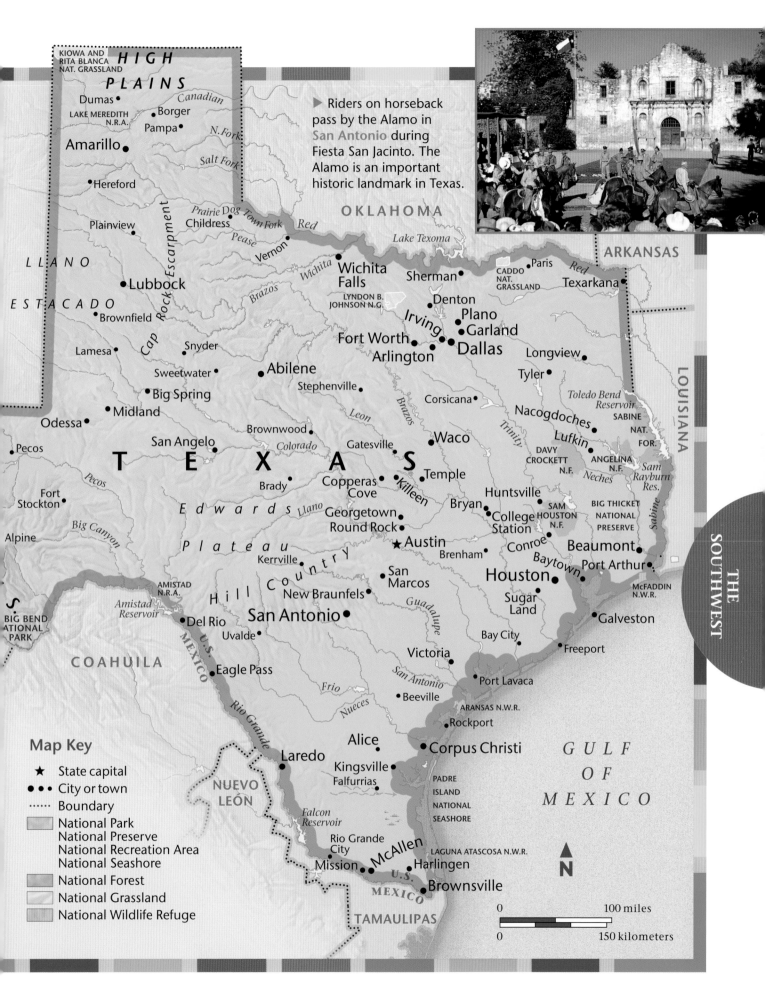

KIOWA AND
RITA BLANCA
NAT. GRASSLAND

HIGH
PLAINS

Dumas
Canadian
LAKE MEREDITH
N.R.A.
Borger
Pampa
N. Fork
Amarillo

Hereford

Salt Fork

Plainview

LLANO

Childress
Prairie Dog Town Fork
Red
Pease
Vernon

OKLAHOMA

Lake Texoma

Riders on horseback
pass by the Alamo in
San Antonio during
Fiesta San Jacinto. The
Alamo is an important
historic landmark in Texas.

ARKANSAS

Paris
Red
CADDO
NAT.
GRASSLAND
Texarkana

ESTACADO

Lubbock

Brownfield

Lamesa

Snyder

Sweetwater

Big Spring

Odessa

Midland

Pecos

Pecos

Fort
Stockton

Big Canyon

Alpine

BIG BEND
ATIONAL
PARK

Cap Rock Escarpment

Brazos
Wichita
Wichita
Falls
LYNDON B.
JOHNSON N.G.

Sherman

Denton

Irving
Plano
Fort Worth
Garland
Arlington
Dallas

Longview

Abilene
Tyler

Stephenville

Corsicana
Nacogdoches
Toledo Bend
Reservoir
SABINE
NAT.
FOR.

LOUISIANA

T E X A S

Brownwood
Leon
Brazos

Waco

Lufkin

San Angelo
Colorado
Gatesville
Temple
DAVY
CROCKETT
N.F.
ANGELINA
N.F.
Sam
Rayburn
Res.

Brady
Copperas
Cove
Killeen
Bryan
Huntsville
SAM
HOUSTON
N.F.
BIG THICKET
NATIONAL
PRESERVE

Edwards
Llano
Georgetown
Round Rock
College
Station
Neches
Sabine

Plateau
Austin
Brenham
Conroe
Beaumont

Kerrville
Country
Baytown
Port Arthur

AMISTAD
N.R.A.
Hill
New Braunfels
San
Marcos
Houston
McFADDIN
N.W.R.

Amistad
Reservoir
Del Rio
San Antonio
Guadalupe
Sugar
Land

Uvalde
Bay City
Galveston

COAHUILA

MEXICO
U.S.
Eagle Pass
Frio
Nueces
San Antonio
Victoria
Port Lavaca
Freeport

Beeville
ARANSAS N.W.R.
Rockport

Map Key

★ State capital
••• City or town
⋯⋯ Boundary

National Park
National Preserve
National Recreation Area
National Seashore
National Forest
National Grassland
National Wildlife Refuge

Rio Grande

NUEVO
LEÓN

Laredo

Alice

Kingsville
Falfurrias

Corpus Christi

PADRE
ISLAND
NATIONAL
SEASHORE

GULF
OF
MEXICO

Falcon
Reservoir

Rio Grande
City
McAllen
Mission
U.S.
MEXICO
Harlingen
Brownsville

LAGUNA ATASCOSA N.W.R.

N

TAMAULIPAS

0   100 miles

0   150 kilometers

The West

The West region makes up almost half of the landmass of the U.S. The region's varied landscapes and climates range from the frozen heights of Denali in Alaska, to the barren desert of Death Valley in California and the lush tropical forests of Hawai'i. More than half the region's people live in California. The Los Angeles metropolitan area is second only to that of New York City in the Northeast. Other parts of the region have few people, and much of the land is set aside as parkland and military bases.

The snowy peaks of Maroon Bells-Snowmass Wilderness near Aspen, Colorado, rise over 14,000 feet (4,200 m). Mountains—the Rockies, Tetons, and Sierra Nevadas—are important landscape features of the West, and provide habitat for mountain lions and other wildlife.

The West

California

![river icon] **Land & Water** The Sierra Nevadas, the Mojave Desert, and San Francisco Bay are important land and water features of California.

![flags icon] **Statehood** California became the 31st state in 1850.

![people icon] **People & Places** California's population is 36,756,666. Sacramento is the state capital. The largest city is Los Angeles.

![question mark icon] **Fun Fact** Death Valley is the hottest place in the U.S. In July 1913, what is now Furnace Creek Ranch registered a temperature of 134°F (57°C).

▶ Stretching more than a mile (1.6 km) across the entrance to San Francisco Bay, the Golden Gate Bridge opened in 1937.

▲ An elephant seal on one of California's Channel Islands roars at a photographer who has invaded the seal's territory on the beach.

▼ Automobiles can drive through the base of this California redwood tree in Leggett, nicknamed the "Chandelier Tree" because of its huge branches.

California State Flag

Golden Poppy
State Flower

California Quail
State Bird

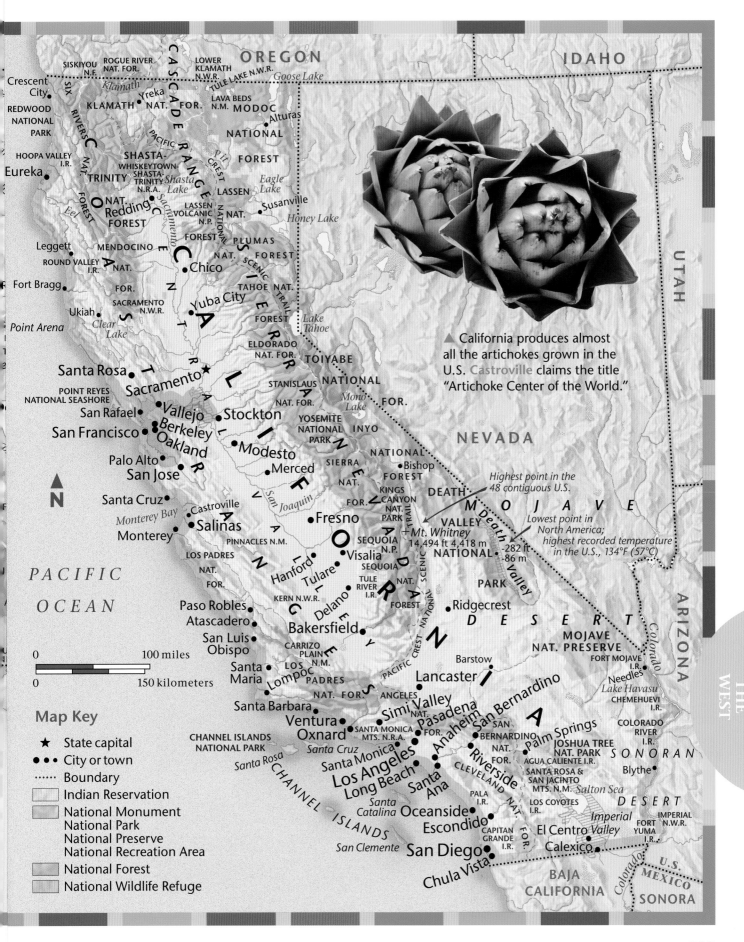

OREGON   IDAHO

Crescent
City
REDWOOD
NATIONAL
PARK

HOOPA VALLEY
I.R.

Eureka

Leggett
ROUND VALLEY
I.R.
Fort Bragg

Ukiah

Point Arena

SISKIYOU
N.F.
ROGUE RIVER
NAT. FOR.

LOWER
KLAMATH
N.W.R.
TULE LAKE N.W.R.   *Goose Lake*

Klamath
KLAMATH   Yreka
NAT. FOR.

Klamath

SHASTA-
WHISKEYTOWN-
SHASTA-
TRINITY
N.R.A.
Shasta Lake

ONAT.
Redding
FOREST

MENDOCINO
NAT.
FOR.

Eel

Clear Lake

LAVA BEDS
N.M. MODOC
Alturas
NATIONAL
FOREST

LASSEN
NAT.
LASSEN
VOLCANIC
N.P.

Eagle Lake

Susanville

Honey Lake

PLUMAS
NAT.   FOREST

Chico

TAHOE NAT.
FOREST

Lake Tahoe

ELDORADO
NAT. FOR.

TOIYABE

Yuba City

Santa Rosa
POINT REYES
NATIONAL SEASHORE
San Rafael
San Francisco Berkeley
Oakland
Palo Alto
San Jose

Sacramento
Vallejo   Stockton

Modesto
Merced

STANISLAUS
NAT. FOR.

Mono Lake

NATIONAL

FOR.

YOSEMITE
NATIONAL
PARK

NEVADA

California produces almost
all the artichokes grown in the
U.S. Castroville claims the title
"Artichoke Center of the World."

INYO

NATIONAL

Bishop
FOREST

Santa Cruz
Castroville
Monterey Bay
Salinas
Monterey
PINNACLES N.M.
LOS PADRES
NAT.
FOR.

Paso Robles
Atascadero
San Luis
Obispo
Santa
Maria
Lompoc

Santa Barbara

CARRIZO
PLAIN
N.M.

LOS
PADRES
NAT. FOR.

SIERRA
NAT.

FOR.
San Joaquin
KINGS
CANYON
NAT. PARK

Fresno

Hanford
Tulare
Delano

Visalia
SEQUOIA
N.P.
TULE
RIVER
I.R.

KERN N.W.R.
Bakersfield

ANGELES
NAT.
FOR.

DEATH

VALLEY

Mt. Whitney
14,494 ft 4,418 m

Highest point in the
48 contiguous U.S.

SEQUOIA

NAT.

FOREST

NATIONAL

PARK

Ridgecrest

MOJAVE

Lowest point in
North America;
highest recorded temperature
in the U.S., 134°F (57°C)

-282 ft
-86 m

DESERT

MOJAVE
NAT. PRESERVE

Barstow

UTAH

ARIZONA

Colorado

FORT MOJAVE
I.R.
Needles
Lake Havasu
CHEMEHUEVI
I.R.

COLORADO
RIVER
I.R.

PACIFIC

OCEAN

0   100 miles

0   150 kilometers

Map Key

★   State capital
••• City or town
···· Boundary
     Indian Reservation
     National Monument
     National Park
     National Preserve
     National Recreation Area
     National Forest
     National Wildlife Refuge

CHANNEL ISLANDS
NATIONAL PARK

Santa Cruz

Santa Rosa

CHANNEL ISLANDS

*Santa
Catalina*

San Clemente

Ventura
Oxnard
SANTA MONICA
MTS. N.R.A.
Santa Monica

Los Angeles
Long Beach

Simi Valley
Pasadena

Anaheim
Santa
Ana

Oceanside

Escondido

San Diego

Chula Vista

Lancaster

San Bernardino

SAN
BERNARDINO
NAT.
FOR.
Riverside
CLEVELAND
NAT.
FOR.
PALA
I.R.
CAPITAN
GRANDE
I.R.

Palm Springs

JOSHUA TREE
NAT. PARK
AGUA CALIENTE I.R.
SANTA ROSA &
SAN JACINTO
MTS. N.M. *Salton Sea*
LOS COYOTES
I.R.

SONORAN

Blythe

COLORADO
RIVER
I.R.

DESERT

Imperial
Valley

El Centro

Calexico

FORT
YUMA
I.R.

IMPERIAL
N.W.R.

BAJA
CALIFORNIA

Colorado

U.S.
MEXICO

SONORA

THE
WEST

The West

Hawai'i

Land & Water Kilauea crater, Diamond Head, and Pearl Harbor are important land and water features of Hawai'i.

Statehood Hawai'i became the 50th state in 1959.

People & Places Hawai'i's population is 1,288,198. Honolulu is the state capital and the largest city.

Fun Fact Hawai'i is the fastest growing state in the U.S.—not in people, but in land. Active volcanoes are constantly creating new land as lava continues to flow.

◀ Pu'u 'O'o vent on **Kilauea crater** has added more than 568 acres (230 ha) of new land to Hawai'i.

KAUA'I

Wai'ale'ale
5,148 ft
1,569 m

WAIMEA
CANYON

Kaulakahi Channel

Lehua I.

Pu'uwai

Kekaha

Kalaheo

Lihu'e

Kapa'a

NI'IHAU

Kaua

PACIFIC

▼ Hawai'i is the leading pineapple producer in the U.S. Pineapples are grown on **Lana'i, Maui,** and **O'ahu.**

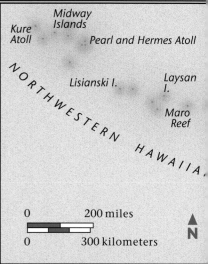

Midway Islands

Kure Atoll

Pearl and Hermes Atoll

NORTHWESTERN HAWAIIAN

Lisianski I.

Laysan I.

Maro Reef

0   200 miles

0   300 kilometers

N

Hawai'i State Flag

Hibiscus State Flower

Hawaiian Goose (Nene) State Bird

◀ A surfer balances on his board. People travel great distances to ride the big waves off the North Shore of O'ahu.

▶ A young girl performs a traditional Polynesian hula on a misty day in Waimea Canyon on the island of Kaua'i.

▶ Green sea turtles migrate 800 miles (1,287 km) to their nesting area in the Northwestern Hawaiian Islands.

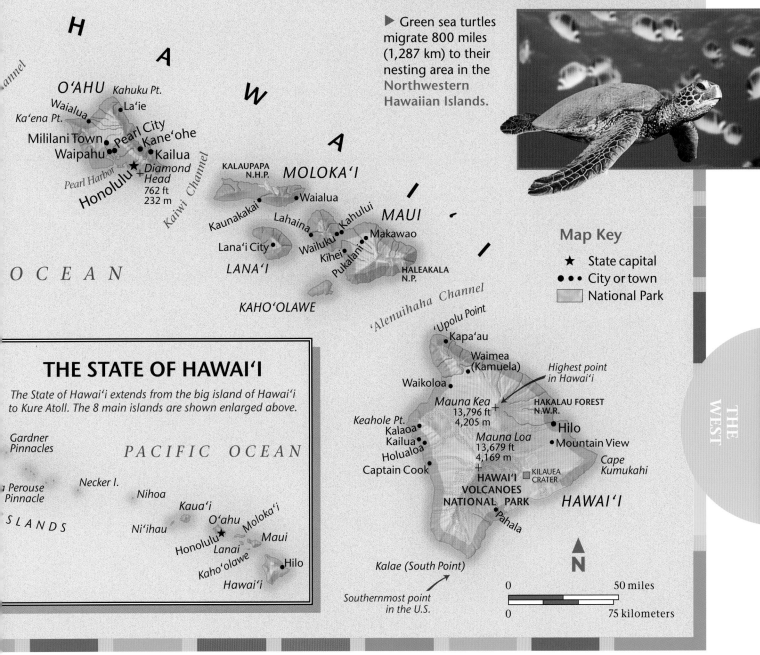

H A W A I I

O'AHU
Kahuku Pt.
Waialua
La'ie
Ka'ena Pt.
Mililani Town
Pearl City
Kane'ohe
Waipahu
Kailua
Pearl Harbor
Honolulu
Diamond Head
762 ft
232 m
Kaiwi Channel

annel

OCEAN

KALAUPAPA N.H.P.
MOLOKA'I
Waialua
Kaunakakai
Lahaina
Kahului
MAUI
Lana'i City
Wailuku
Makawao
Kihei
Pukalani
LANA'I
HALEAKALA N.P.

KAHO'OLAWE

'Alenuihaha Channel

Map Key
★ State capital
••• City or town
▢ National Park

THE STATE OF HAWAI'I

The State of Hawai'i extends from the big island of Hawai'i to Kure Atoll. The 8 main islands are shown enlarged above.

Gardner Pinnacles

a Perouse Pinnacle

PACIFIC OCEAN

Necker I.

Nihoa

Ni'ihau

Kaua'i

O'ahu

Moloka'i

Honolulu

Lanai

Maui

Kaho'olawe

Hawai'i

Hilo

SLANDS

'Upolu Point
Kapa'au
Waimea (Kamuela)
Highest point in Hawai'i
Waikoloa
Mauna Kea
13,796 ft
4,205 m
HAKALAU FOREST N.W.R.
Keahole Pt.
Kalaoa
Mauna Loa
13,679 ft
4,169 m
Hilo
Kailua
Mountain View
Holualoa
Cape Kumukahi
Captain Cook
KILAUEA CRATER
HAWAI'I
VOLCANOES
NATIONAL PARK
HAWAI'I
Pahala

Kalae (South Point)

Southernmost point in the U.S.

0   50 miles
0   75 kilometers

N

The West

▲ A wood duck perches on a post. These colorful waterfowl can be viewed in Kootenai National Wildlife Refuge near **Bonners Ferry**.

Idaho

 Land & Water The Bitterroot Range, the Columbia Plateau, and the Snake River are important land and water features of Idaho.

Statehood Idaho became the 43rd state in 1890.

People & Places Idaho's population is 1,523,816. Boise is the state capital and the largest city.

Fun Fact In preparation for their mission to the moon, Apollo astronauts visited Craters of the Moon National Monument and Preserve to study its volcanic geology and experience its harsh environment.

▲ More than 40 percent of Idaho's land area is forested. Use of this land is overseen by the Forest Products Commission in **Boise.** Forest products are important to the state's economy.

Idaho State Flag

Syringa (Mock Orange) State Flower

Mountain Bluebird State Bird

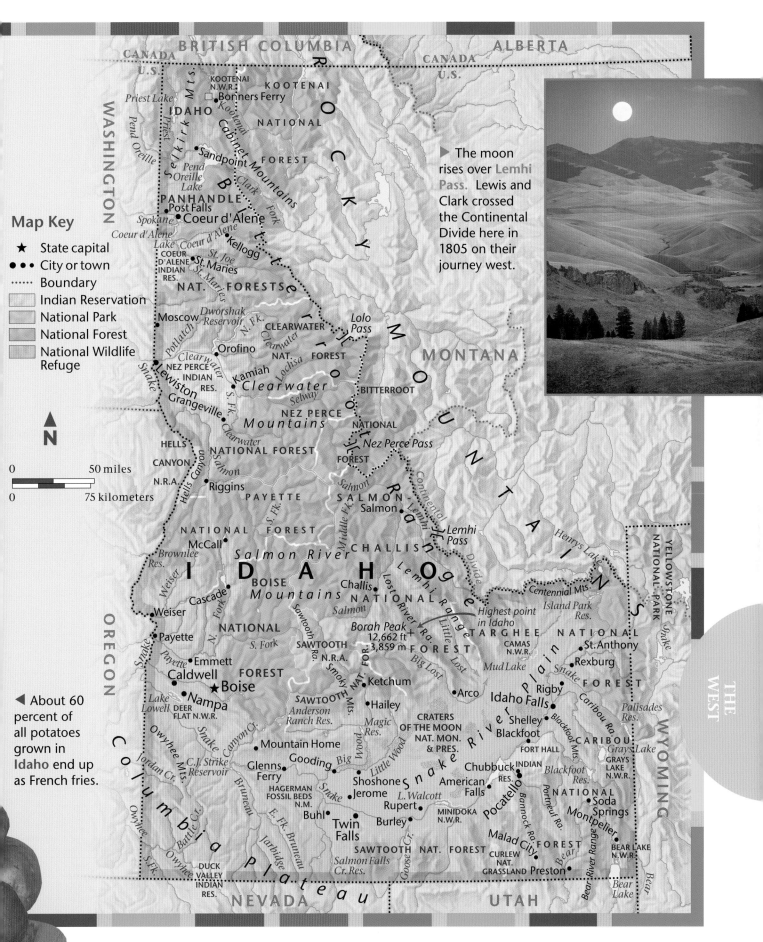

Map Key

★ State capital
• • • City or town
⋯⋯ Boundary
☐ Indian Reservation
National Park
National Forest
National Wildlife Refuge

N

0 — 50 miles
0 — 75 kilometers

▶ The moon rises over **Lemhi Pass.** Lewis and Clark crossed the Continental Divide here in 1805 on their journey west.

◀ About 60 percent of all potatoes grown in **Idaho** end up as French fries.

CANADA / U.S.
BRITISH COLUMBIA
ALBERTA
CANADA / U.S.

WASHINGTON

KOOTENAI N.W.R.
☐ Bonners Ferry
KOOTENAI
Priest Lake
IDAHO
NATIONAL
Kootenai
Priest
Selkirk Mts.
Cabinet Mountains
FOREST
ROCKY

Pend Oreille
Sandpoint
Clark Fork
Pend Oreille Lake
PANHANDLE
Post Falls
Spokane
Coeur d'Alene
Coeur d'Alene Lake
Kellogg
COEUR D'ALENE INDIAN RES.
St. Joe
Coeur d'Alene
St. Joe
NAT. FORESTS
St. Maries
St. Maries

Moscow
Dworshak Reservoir
N. Fk.
CLEARWATER
Lolo Pass
Bitterroot
MONTANA

Clearwater
Potlatch
Clearwater
Orofino
NAT. FOREST
Lochsa
Clearwater

Lewiston
NEZ PERCE INDIAN RES.
Kamiah
S. Fk.
Clearwater
Selway
BITTERROOT
Snake
Clearwater
Grangeville
NEZ PERCE
Mountains
NATIONAL
Nez Perce Pass
HELLS
NATIONAL FOREST
FOREST
CANYON
Salmon
Hells Canyon
N.R.A.
Riggins
PAYETTE
Salmon
Salmon
SALMON-
CHALLIS
Continental
Lemhi

Brownlee Res.
Weiser
McCall
NATIONAL FOREST
S. Fk.
Salmon River
Salmon
Lemhi Pass
Henrys Lake
Divide
YELLOWSTONE NATIONAL PARK
Snake

IDAHO
BOISE
Cascade
Challis
NATIONAL
Centennial Mts.
Island Park Res.
Mountains
Salmon
Weiser
N. Fork
Sawtooth Ra.
Lost River
Highest point in Idaho
TARGHEE
NATIONAL
CAMAS N.W.R.
Mud Lake
Snake
St. Anthony
Rexburg
FOREST

OREGON
Payette
NATIONAL
S. Fork
Borah Peak 12,662 ft 3,859 m
Little Lost
FOREST
Big Lost
Rigby
Caribou Ra.
Palisades Res.

Emmett
SAWTOOTH
Smoky Mts.
NAT. FOR.
Ketchum
Idaho Falls
Snake River Plain
Caldwell
FOREST
N.R.A.
Hailey
Shelley
Caribou
Payette
Boise
SAWTOOTH Mts.
Arco
Blackfoot
CARIBOU
Lake Lowell
Nampa
DEER FLAT N.W.R.
Anderson Ranch Res.
Magic Res.
CRATERS OF THE MOON NAT. MON. & PRES.
FORT HALL
Grays Lake
GRAYS LAKE N.W.R.
Wood
Big Wood
Little Wood
Chubbuck INDIAN RES.
Blackfoot Mts.
Blackfoot Res.
Owyhee Mts.
Mountain Home
C.J. Strike Reservoir
Gooding
Shoshone
American Falls
NATIONAL
Soda Springs
Canyon Cr.
Glenns Ferry
Bruneau
Jerome
L. Walcott
Pocatello
Portneuf Ra.
FOREST
Montpelier
Jordan Cr.
HAGERMAN FOSSIL BEDS N.M.
Snake
Rupert
MINIDOKA N.W.R.
Bannock Ra.
Bear
Buhl
Burley
Goose Cr.
Malad City
CURLEW NAT. GRASSLAND
Bear River Range
BEAR LAKE N.W.R.
Battle Cr.
Twin Falls
SAWTOOTH NAT. FOREST
Soda Springs
Preston
Bear
Bear Lake

Owyhee
Jarbidge
E. Fk. Bruneau
Salmon Falls Cr. Res.
S. Fk.
DUCK VALLEY INDIAN RES.

Columbia Plateau
WYOMING

NEVADA
UTAH

THE WEST

The West

Montana

Land & Water The Rocky Mountains, Great Plains, and the Yellowstone River are important land and water features of Montana.

Statehood Montana became the 41st state in 1889.

People & Places Montana's population is 967,440. Helena is the state capital. The largest city is Billings.

Fun Fact Montana is the only state with river systems that empty into the Gulf of Mexico to the southeast, Hudson Bay to the north, and the Pacific Ocean to the west.

MONTANA

Montana State Flag

Bitterroot
State Flower

Western Meadowlark
State Bird

▲ Skiers ride a chairlift up a snowy mountain slope in Whitefish.

▼ Rugged peaks of the Northern Rocky Mountains are reflected in the still surface of a mountain lake in Glacier National Park.

SASKATCHEWAN

CANADA
U.S.

CANADA
U.S.

t Bank

•Shelby

Milk •Chinook

•Havre

Plentywood
•Scobey

MEDICINE LAKE
N.W.R.

*Lake
Elwell*

Marias

•Conrad

ROCKY BOYS
I.R.

FORT
BELKNAP
INDIAN
RESERVATION

•Malta

BOWDOIN
N.W.R.

Milk

•Glasgow

FORT PECK

INDIAN RESERVATION

•Wolf Point

Missouri

NORTH DAKOTA

Teton

Choteau •Fort Benton *Missouri*

BENTON LAKE
N.W.R.

UPPER MISSOURI
RIVER BREAKS N.M.

UL BEND
N.W.R.

Fort Peck Lake

CHARLES M. RUSSELL NAT. WILDLIFE REFUGE

•Sidney

Yellowstone

Sun

Great Falls•

LEWIS

•Jordan

•Circle

AND CLARK

•Lewistown

M O N T A N A

•Glendive

•Wibaux

TIONAL

•Helena

NATIONAL

LAKE
MASON
N.W.R.

•Terry

Canyon Ferry L.

FOREST

•Townsend

FOREST

•Harlowton

•Roundup

Musselshell

•Miles City

•Baker

G R E A T

P L A I N S

Missouri

GALLATIN •Big Timber

•Bozeman •Livingston

NATIONAL

•Columbus

Jefferson

Gallatin

Madison

Virginia City•

FOREST

Absaroka Range

Granite Peak
12,799 ft
3,901 m
+

•Billings

•Laurel

•Red Lodge

Clarks Fk.

CUSTER NAT. FOR.

Yellowstone

Hardin•
Crow Agency•

CROW INDIAN
RESERVATION

BIGHORN CANYON
N.R.A.

Highest point
in Montana

•Forsyth

•Colstrip

Bighorn

Tongue

NORTHERN
CHEYENNE
I.R.

CUSTER NATIONAL FOREST

Powder

•Broadus

Little Missouri

SOUTH DAKOTA

ED ROCK
ES N.W.R.

Yellowstone
Divide

West

YELLOWSTONE

Yellowstone

NATIONAL

I N S

PARK

World's first national
park, 1872

*Bighorn
Mountains*

WYOMING

0   50 miles

0   75 kilometers

N

Map Key

★ State capital

••• City or town

····· Boundary

Indian Reservation

National Monument
National Park
National Preserve
National Recreation Area

National Forest

National Wildlife Refuge

▶ Many people
want the experi-
ence of living
on a ranch. One
family-oriented
ranch near
Bozeman has
special programs
for children.

▼ American bison are protected
in the National Bison Range
Refuge near Moiese.

Nevada

Land & Water
The Great Basin, the Mojave Desert, and Lake Tahoe are important land and water features of Nevada.

Statehood
Nevada became the 36th state in 1864.

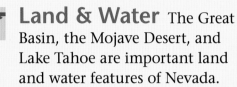
People & Places
Nevada's population is 2,600,167. Carson City is the state capital. The largest city is Las Vegas.

Fun Fact
Between 1975 and 2000, the population of Clark County, home of Las Vegas, grew almost 250 percent. It is still one of the fastest-growing counties in the United States.

▲ The Luxor, recreating a scene from ancient Egypt, is one of many hotel-casinos that attract thousands of tourists to Las Vegas.

◀ Paiute Indians, dressed in traditional clothing, live on the Pyramid Lake Reservation near Reno. Their economy centers on fishing and recreational activities.

▼ The desert environment of Nevada includes many plants that tolerate very dry conditions. The setting sun highlights mountains in the distance.

Nevada State Flag

Mountain Bluebird
State Bird

Sagebrush
State Flower

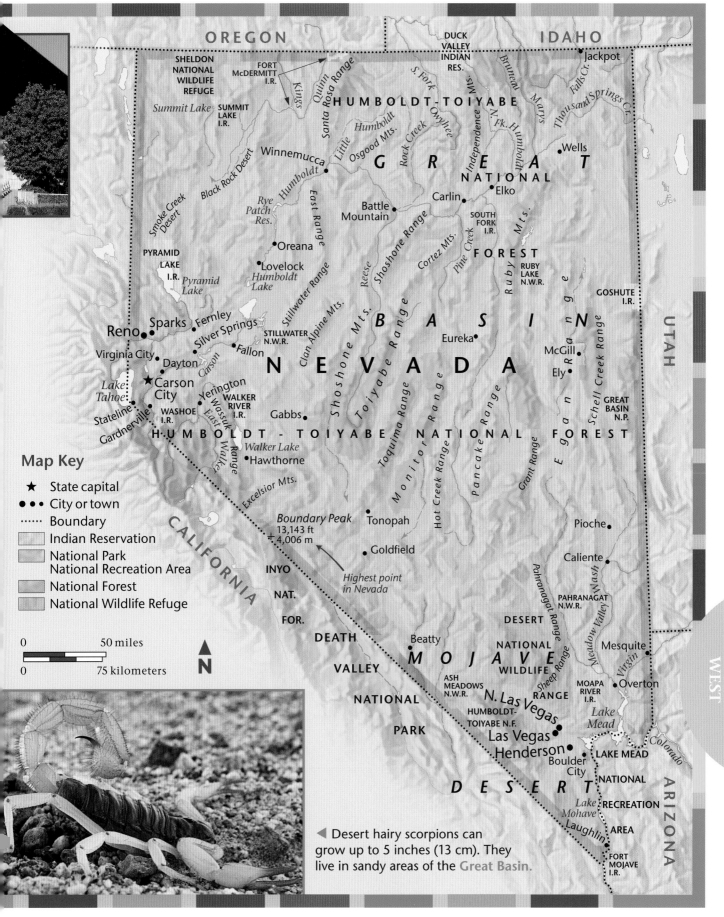

OREGON IDAHO

SHELDON
NATIONAL
WILDLIFE
REFUGE

FORT
McDERMITT
I.R.

DUCK
VALLEY
INDIAN
RES.

Jackpot

Summit Lake

SUMMIT
LAKE
I.R.

HUMBOLDT-TOIYABE

Kings

Quinn

Santa Rosa Range

S. Fork Owyhee

Bruneau

Marys

Thousand Springs Cr.

Falls Cr.

Humboldt

Little

Osgood Mts.

Rock Creek

Independence Mts.

N. Fk. Humboldt

Wells

G R E A T

Winnemucca

Humboldt

East Range

Battle
Mountain

Carlin

Elko

NATIONAL

Black Rock Desert

Smoke Creek Desert

Rye
Patch
Res.

Shoshone Range

Reese

Cortez Mts.

Pine Creek

Ruby Mts.

RUBY
LAKE
N.W.R.

SOUTH
FORK
I.R.

F O R E S T

PYRAMID
LAKE
I.R.

Oreana

Lovelock
Humboldt
Lake

Stillwater Range

Clan Alpine Mts.

Toiyabe Range

GOSHUTE
I.R.

Pyramid
Lake

B A S I N

Eureka

McGill

Schell Creek Range

Egan Range

UTAH

Reno Sparks Fernley

Silver Springs

STILLWATER
N.W.R.

Shoshone Mts.

N E V A D A

Ely

Virginia City

Dayton

Carson

Fallon

Lake
Tahoe

★ Carson
City

Yerington

WALKER
RIVER
I.R.

Gabbs

Toquima Range

Monitor Range

Hot Creek Range

Pancake Range

Grant Range

GREAT
BASIN
N.P.

Stateline

Gardnerville

WASHOE
I.R.

Wassuk Range

East Walker

H U M B O L D T - T O I Y A B E   N A T I O N A L   F O R E S T

Walker Lake

Hawthorne

Excelsior Mts.

Map Key

★ State capital
••• City or town
· · · · Boundary
▢ Indian Reservation
▢ National Park
   National Recreation Area
▢ National Forest
▢ National Wildlife Refuge

0 ——— 50 miles
0 ——— 75 kilometers

▲
N

CALIFORNIA

Boundary Peak
13,143 ft
4,006 m

Tonopah

Highest point
in Nevada

Goldfield

Pioche

Caliente

INYO

NAT.

FOR.

DEATH

Beatty

MOJAVE

DESERT

NATIONAL

WILDLIFE

Pahranagat Range

PAHRANAGAT
N.W.R.

Meadow Valley Wash

Mesquite

VALLEY

ASH
MEADOWS
N.W.R.

Sheep Range

RANGE

MOAPA
RIVER
I.R.

Virgin

Overton

NATIONAL

N. Las Vegas
HUMBOLDT-
TOIYABE N.F.

Lake
Mead

PARK

Las Vegas
Henderson
Boulder
City

LAKE MEAD

Colorado

D E S E R T

Lake
Mohave

NATIONAL

RECREATION

ARIZONA

Laughlin

AREA

FORT
MOJAVE
I.R.

◀ Desert hairy scorpions can
grow up to 5 inches (13 cm). They
live in sandy areas of the Great Basin.

Oregon

Land & Water The Cascade Range, Crater Lake, and the Columbia River are important land and water features of Oregon.

Statehood Oregon became the 33rd state in 1859.

People & Places Oregon's population is 3,790,060. Salem is the state capital. The largest city is Portland.

Fun Fact The Bonneville Power Administration, headquartered in Portland, provides about 45 percent of the electricity used in the Pacific Northwest. Most of this power comes from hydroelectric plants along the Columbia River.

▲ The 125-foot (38-m) Astoria Column near the mouth of the Columbia River is covered with scenes of historic events.

▲ The cool, moist climate of the valley of the Willamette River is well-suited to certain varieties of wine grapes.

▼ Rocky outcrops called sea stacks line Oregon's Pacific coast. They are remains of a former coastline that has been eroded by waves.

Oregon State Flag

STATE OF OREGON
1859

Oregon Grape State Flower

Western Meadowlark State Bird

Map labels: Astoria, Seaside, Nehalem, PACIFIC OCEAN, Tillamook, Trask, Lincoln City, SIUSLAW, Dal, Newport, NATIONAL, Florence, FOREST, Siusl, OREGON DUNES N.R.A., Reedsport, Umpqua, Coos Bay, North Bend, Sutherli, Coos Bay, Coos, Coquille, Rosebu, Cape Blanco, SISKIYOU, Rogue, Grant Pas, Gold Beach, NATIONAL, Chetco, Illinos, Brookings, FOREST, KLAMA

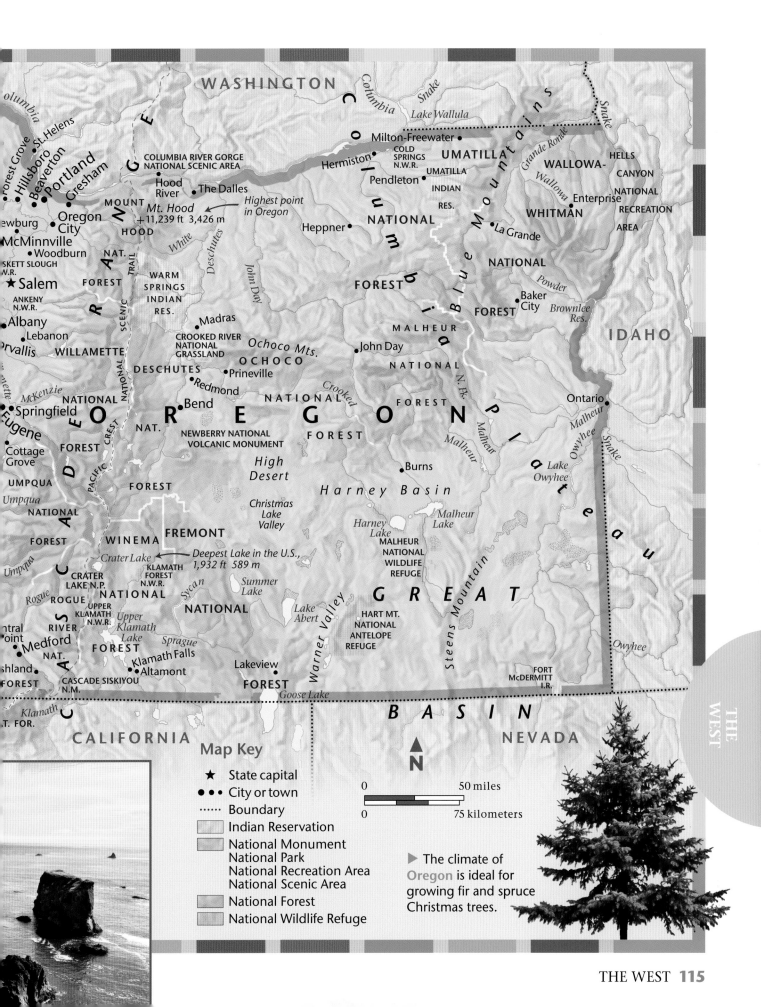

WASHINGTON

COLUMBIA RANGE

Columbia

Snake

Lake Wallula

Snake

Forest Grove
St. Helens
Hillsboro
Beaverton
Portland
Gresham

COLUMBIA RIVER GORGE
NATIONAL SCENIC AREA

Hood
River

The Dalles

Milton-Freewater

Hermiston

COLD
SPRINGS
N.W.R.

UMATILLA

UMATILLA

Pendleton

INDIAN

RES.

MOUNT

Mt. Hood
+11,239 ft 3,426 m

Highest point
in Oregon

NATIONAL

wburg
Oregon
City

HOOD

Blue Mountains

WALLOWA-

HELLS

CANYON

NATIONAL

Enterprise

RECREATION

AREA

McMinnville

NAT.

White

Heppner

La Grande

WHITMAN

Grande Ronde

Woodburn

KETT SLOUGH
W.R.

★ Salem

FOREST

Deschutes

FOREST

NATIONAL

Powder

ANKENY
N.W.R.

WARM
SPRINGS
INDIAN
RES.

John Day

MALHEUR

FOREST

Baker
City

Brownlee
Res.

Albany

Lebanon

Madras

NATIONAL

IDAHO

rvallis

WILLAMETTE

CROOKED RIVER
NATIONAL
GRASSLAND

Ochoco Mts.

John Day

mette

McKenzie

DESCHUTES

OCHOCO

Prineville

FOREST

N. Fk.

Springfield

NATIONAL

Redmond

Crooked

FOREST

Ontario

Malheur

Eugene

FOREST

Bend

NATIONAL

Malheur

Malheur

Cottage
Grove

NAT.

NEWBERRY NATIONAL
VOLCANIC MONUMENT

FOREST

Burns

UMPQUA

High
Desert

Harney Basin

Lake
Owyhee

Owyhee

Snake

Umpqua

FOREST

Christmas
Lake
Valley

Malheur
Lake

NATIONAL

WINEMA

FREMONT

Harney
Lake

MALHEUR

Umpqua

Crater Lake

Deepest Lake in the U.S.,
1,932 ft 589 m

NATIONAL
WILDLIFE
REFUGE

FOREST

KLAMATH
FOREST
N.W.R.

Sycan

Summer
Lake

CRATER
LAKE N.P.

NATIONAL

GREAT

ROGUE

UPPER
KLAMATH
N.W.R.

Upper
Klamath
Lake

Lake
Abert

Steens Mountain

RIVER

HART MT.
NATIONAL
ANTELOPE
REFUGE

Medford

FOREST

Sprague

Warner Valley

Owyhee

NAT.

Klamath Falls

Altamont

hland

CASCADE SISKIYOU
N.M.

Lakeview

FOREST

FORT
McDERMITT
I.R.

FOREST

Rogue

CASCADE

Goose Lake

BASIN

Klamath
T. FOR.

CALIFORNIA

NEVADA

N

Map Key

★ State capital

••• City or town

········ Boundary

Indian Reservation

National Monument
National Park
National Recreation Area
National Scenic Area

National Forest

National Wildlife Refuge

0   50 miles

0   75 kilometers

► The climate of
Oregon is ideal for
growing fir and spruce
Christmas trees.

The West

Utah

Land & Water The Great Basin, the Uinta Mountains, and the Great Salt Lake are important land and water features of Utah.

Statehood Utah became the 45th state in 1896.

People & Places Utah's population is 2,736,424. Salt Lake City is the state capital and the largest city.

Fun Fact Great Salt Lake is the largest natural lake west of the Mississippi River. The lake, which has a high level of evaporation, is about eight times saltier than the ocean.

▲ Water sports such as inner tubing are popular activities in the Glen Canyon National Recreation Area.

◄ A newly married couple stands in front of the Temple in Salt Lake City, where Mormons gather for religious ceremonies.

▼ Arches National Park includes more than 2,000 arches carved by natural forces over millions of years. Delicate Arch stands on the canyon edge, with the La Sal Mountains in the distance.

Utah State Flag

Sego Lilly

California Gull State Bird

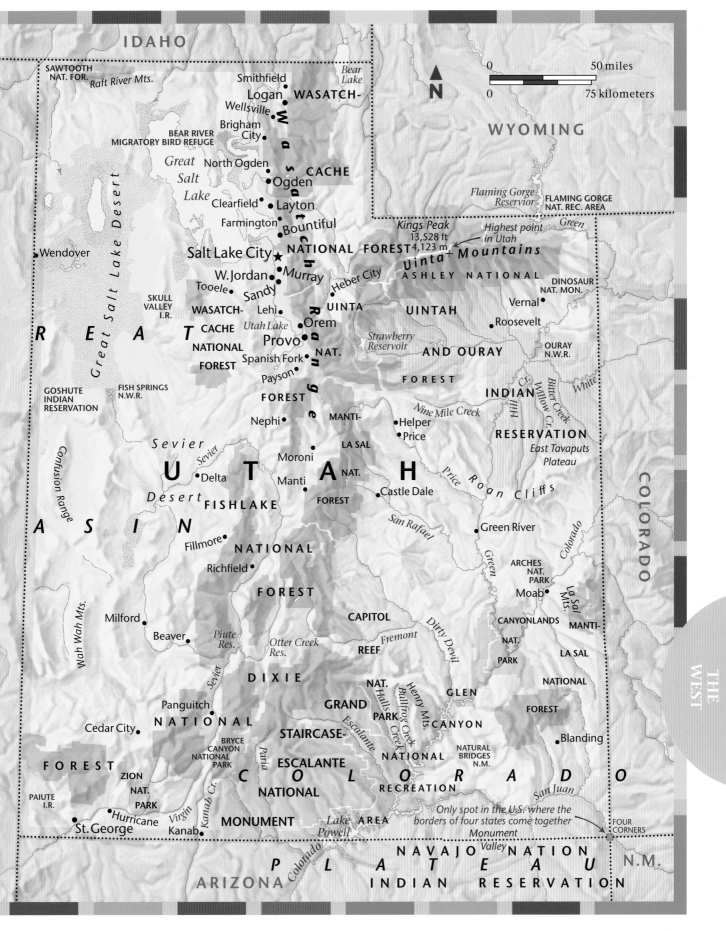

IDAHO

SAWTOOTH
NAT. FOR.   *Raft River Mts.*

Smithfield •
*Bear
Lake*

Logan • **WASATCH-**

Wellsville •

Brigham
City •

BEAR RIVER
MIGRATORY BIRD REFUGE

*Great
Salt
Lake*

North Ogden • **CACHE**

Ogden •

Clearfield • Layton •

Farmington • Bountiful •

• Wendover

Salt Lake City ★ **NATIONAL FOREST**

W. Jordan • • Murray

Tooele • Sandy •

SKULL
VALLEY
I.R.

WASATCH- Lehi •

CACHE *Utah Lake* • Orem

NATIONAL Provo •

FOREST Spanish Fork •

Payson •

GOSHUTE
INDIAN
RESERVATION

FISH SPRINGS
N.W.R.

FOREST

Nephi •

Sevier

U   T   A   H

Sevier

• Delta

FISHLAKE

Desert

Fillmore •

Richfield • **NATIONAL**

FOREST

Milford •

Beaver •

*Piute
Res.*

*Otter Creek
Res.*

Panguitch • **DIXIE**

Cedar City • **NATIONAL**

BRYCE
CANYON
NATIONAL
PARK

STAIRCASE-

FOREST

ZION
NAT.
PARK

PAIUTE
I.R.

• Hurricane

St. George • Kanab •

WYOMING

0   50 miles
0   75 kilometers

N

*Flaming Gorge
Reservoir* FLAMING GORGE
NAT. REC. AREA

*Kings Peak
13,528 ft
4,123 m* Highest point
in Utah *Green*

Uinta + Mountains

ASHLEY   NATIONAL

Heber City • DINOSAUR
NAT. MON.

UINTA **UINTAH** Vernal •

*Strawberry
Reservoir* • Roosevelt

NAT. **AND OURAY** OURAY
N.W.R.

FOREST

INDIAN *White*

Nine Mile Creek **RESERVATION**

MANTI- Helper • *East Tavaputs
Plateau*

• Price

LA SAL

Moroni • **NAT.**

Manti • **FOREST** Castle Dale •

San Rafael

Price *Roan   Cliffs*

• Green River *Colorado*

CAPITOL *Fremont* ARCHES
NAT.
PARK

REEF *Dirty Devil* Moab • *La Sal
Mts.*

GRAND **NAT.** *Halls Creek* *Bullfrog Creek* **GLEN** **CANYONLANDS** **MANTI-**

PARK **NAT.** **LA SAL**

ESCALANTE *Escalante* **CANYON** **PARK** **NATIONAL**

NATIONAL *Henry Mts.* NATURAL
BRIDGES
N.M. **FOREST**

C   O   L   O   R   A   D   O • Blanding

Paria **RECREATION**

MONUMENT *Lake
Powell* **AREA** *San Juan*

Only spot in the U.S. where the
borders of four states come together FOUR
CORNERS

Kanab Cr. *Virgin* Kanab • *Valley* Monument

Colorado **N   A   V   A   J   O** **N   A   T   I   O   N** N.M.

ARIZONA **P   L   A   T   E   A   U** **INDIAN   RESERVATION**

G   R   E   A   T

Great Salt Lake Desert

B   A   S   I   N

Confusion Range

Wah Wah Mts.

N   E   V   A   D   A

C   O   L   O   R   A   D   O

The West

Washington

Land & Water

The Olympic Mountains, the Palouse Hills, and Puget Sound are important land and water features of Washington.

Statehood

Washington became the 42nd state in 1889.

People & Places

Washington's population is 6,549,224. Olympia is the state capital. The largest city is Seattle.

Fun Fact

Mt. Rainier, a dormant volcano, last erupted in 1969. Another nearby volcano, Mt. St. Helens, erupted in 1980. Ash from that eruption was carried by winds as far away as Maine.

▲ A Roosevelt elk grazes in the temperate rain forest of **Olympic National Forest**. Adult males weigh up to 1,000 pounds (454 kg).

◄ **Seattle**'s modern skyline is easily recognized because of its Space Needle tower. The city is an important West Coast port.

Vancouver Island

Cape Flattery
MAKAH I.R.
Strait of Juan de Fuca

Port Angele

Sol Duc
OLYMPIC N.F.

Olympi

OLYMPIC NAT. PAR

Mountain

Queets

QUINAULT INDIAN RES.

FOR

Hoquiam
Aberdeen

Grays Harbor

Willapa Bay

Raymor

WILLAPA N.W.R.

Cape Disappointment

Colum

PACIFIC OCEAN

COAST RANGES

0   50 miles
0   75 kilometers

Washington State Flag

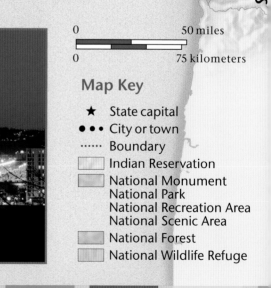

Coast Rhododendron State Flower

American Goldfinch State Bird

Map Key

★ State capital
••• City or town
...... Boundary
◻ Indian Reservation
◻ National Monument
  National Park
  National Recreation Area
  National Scenic Area
◻ National Forest
◻ National Wildlife Refuge

BRITISH COLUMBIA

CANADA
U.S.

CANADA
U.S.
IDAHO

Georgia

LUMMI I.R.
Bellingham

San Juan Islands

Anacortes

Skagit

MOUNT

Mount Vernon

NORTH CASCADES NATIONAL PARK

Ross Lake

ROSS LAKE N.R.A.

LAKE CHELAN N.R.A.

OKANOGAN NATIONAL FOREST

Okanogan

Methow

Republic

Omak

COLVILLE NATIONAL FOREST

Franklin Delano Roosevelt Lake

Colville

LITTLE PEND OREILLE N.W.R.

PANHANDLE

NATIONAL

KALISPELL I.R.

FORESTS

Whidbey Island

Oak Harbor

TULALIP I.R.

BAKER–

WENATCHEE

COLVILLE INDIAN RESERVATION

Sanpoil

RECREATION NATIONAL

Colville

Pend Oreille

Port Townsend

Everett

Lake Chelan

Columbia

Grand Coulee

LAKE ROOSEVELT

SPOKANE INDIAN RES.

Spokane

Opportunity

OLYMPIC NAT.

Bremerton

Kirkland

Skykomish

NATIONAL

SNOQUALMIE

Redmond

Bellevue

Seattle

Renton

NAT.

Auburn

Tacoma

Puyallup

PACIFIC

CREST

FOREST

WASHINGTON

Wenatchee

Yakima

Columbia

Banks Lake

Ephrata

Moses Lake

Potholes Reservoir

COLUMBIA N.W.R.

Ritzville

Palouse

Hills

Medical Lake

TURNBULL N.W.R.

Palouse

Pullman

PUYALLUP I.R.

Shelton

Olympia

Tumwater

Mt. Rainier 14,411 ft 4,392 m

Highest point in Washington

Ellensburg

Naches

SADDLE MT. N.W.R.

Othello

Snake

Pomeroy

Lake Sacajawea

Dayton

Clarkston

Snake

Centralia

Alder Lake

FOREST

MT. RAINIER N.P.

Chehalis

Chehalis

MOUNT BAKER–SNOQUALMIE N.F.

GIFFORD

Cowlitz

PINCHOT

Yakima

Toppenish

YAKAMA

INDIAN

RESERVATION

HANFORD REACH NAT. MON.

Yakima

Prosser

Richland

Kennewick

Pasco

McNARY N.W.R.

Lake Wallula

Walla Walla

UMATILLA

MT. ST. HELENS NAT. VOLCANIC MON.

Kelso

Lewis

NATIONAL

Longview

Vancouver

Camas

COLUMBIA RIVER GORGE NAT. SCENIC AREA

Goldendale

Klickitat

CONBOY LAKE N.W.R.

Columbia

OREGON

Blue Mountains

NATIONAL

FOREST

N

◀ Tulips are big business in the Skagit Valley, where thousands of these colorful flowers burst into bloom every spring.

▲ An orca swims near the San Juan Islands. Also known as killer whales, orcas are really a type of dolphin.

Wyoming

Land & Water
The Rocky Mountains, Yellowstone National Park, and the Green River are important land and water features of Wyoming.

Statehood
Wyoming became the 44th state in 1890.

People & Places
Wyoming's population is 532,668. Cheyenne is the state capital and the largest city.

Fun Fact
Wyoming is called the Equity State because it was the first state to give women the right to vote, granted in 1869 when it was still a territory.

▲ Steam and water from Old Faithful Geyser in **Yellowstone National Park** erupt more than 100 feet (30 m) into the air.

Map Key
- ★ State capital
- ••• City or town
- ······ Boundary
- ▢ Indian Reservation
- ▢ National Monument
  National Park
  National Recreation Area
- ▢ National Forest
- ▢ National Grassland
- ▢ National Wildlife Refuge

Wyoming State Flag

**Indian Paintbrush
State Flower**

**Western Meadowlark
State Bird**

◀ The Wyoming State Capitol building in **Cheyenne** was completed in 1890. It is now a U.S. national historic landmark.

0   50 miles
0   75 kilometers

MONTANA

BIGHORN CANYON N.R.A.

SHOSHONE

Powell
Lovell
Cody
Greybull
Buffalo Bill Reservoir

Bighorn Lake

BIGHORN NATIONAL FOREST

Sheridan
Buffalo

Clear Creek

Powder

GREAT

THUNDER
BLACK
Little Powder
Keyhole Reservoir
Sundance
HILLS
NAT.
FOR.

SOUTH DAKOTA

Black Hills

NATIONAL
FOREST

aroka Range

N. Fork
Shoshone
S. Fork

Greybull

Bighorn

Nowood

Bighorn Mountains

Worland

Gillette

BASIN
Belle Fourche

Newcastle

Wright

NATIONAL

FOREST

Owl Creek

Highest point in Wyoming

Wind

Thermopolis

Middle Fork

S. Fork Powder

GRASSLAND

Cheyenne

Gannett Peak
13,804 ft
4,207 m

WIND RIVER

Wind

INDIAN

Ocean Lake

Boysen Reservoir

W Y O M I N G

RESERVATION
Riverton

Pinedale

Lander
Riverton

Casper

Glenrock
Douglas

Lusk

Niobrara

SHOSHONE

NATIONAL

North Platte

Glendo Reservoir

P

FOREST

Wind River Range

FOREST

Sweetwater

PATHFINDER N.W.R.

L

South Pass
Continental Divide

Pathfinder Reservoir

Guernsey

North Platte

A

Big Sandy

Great Divide
Basin

Seminoe Reservoir

MEDICINE BOW —

Wheatland

Torrington

I

SEEDSKADEE N.W.R.

M
O
U
N
T
A
I
N
S

Medicine Bow

Laramie

N

Green River

Hanna

Medicine Bow

Rock Springs

Rawlins

Continental Divide

North Platte

Saratoga

ROUTT

Horse Cr.

Laramie

S

acks Fork

Medicine Bow Mts.

Front Range

Lodgepole Cr.

ming
Gorge
servoir

FLAMING
GORGE
NATIONAL
RECREATION
AREA

NATIONAL FOREST

Cheyenne ★

THE WEST

Green

COLORADO

NEBRASKA

▶ Unique to **high plains** of the West, the pronghorn can sprint up to 60 miles per hour (97 kph).

◀ The snow-capped peaks of the **Teton Range**, one of the youngest ranges of the West, rise high above a meadow where horses graze.

The Territories

The Territories
ACROSS TWO SEAS

Listed below are the five largest* of the 14 U.S. territories, along with their flags and key information. Two of these are in the Caribbean Sea, and the other three are in the Pacific Ocean. Can you find the other nine U.S. territories on the map?

U.S. CARIBBEAN TERRITORIES

PUERTO RICO

Area: 3,508 sq mi (9,086 sq km)

Population: 3,929,000

Capital: San Juan
Population 2,605,000

Languages: Spanish, English

U.S. VIRGIN ISLANDS

Area: 149 sq mi (386 sq km)

Population: 109,000

Capital: Charlotte Amalie
Population 52,000

Languages: English, Spanish or Spanish Creole, French or French Creole

U.S. PACIFIC TERRITORIES

AMERICAN SAMOA

Area: 77 sq mi (199 sq km)

Population: 67,000

Capital: Pago Pago
Population 55,000

Language: Samoan

NORTHERN MARIANA ISLANDS

Area: 184 sq mi (477 sq km)

Population: 82,000

Capital: Saipan
Population 75,000

Languages: Philippine languages, Chinese, Chamorro, English

GUAM

Area: 217 sq mi (561 sq km)

Population: 171,000

Capital: Hagåtña (Agana)
Population 144,000

Languages: English, Chamorro, Philippine languages

OTHER U.S. TERRITORIES

Baker Island, Howland Island, Jarvis Island, Johnston Atoll, Kingman Reef, Midway Islands, Navassa Island, Palmyra Atoll, Wake Island

*Close-up views of the five largest territories are highlighted in pull-out maps and labeled with a letter. You can see where each territory is located by looking for its corresponding letter on the main map.

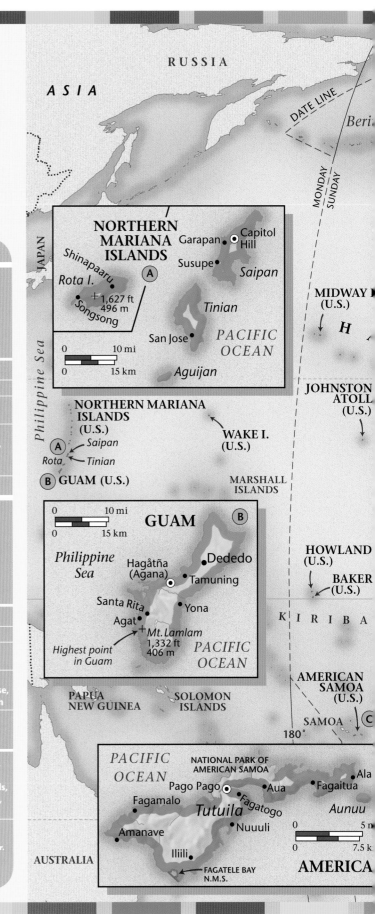

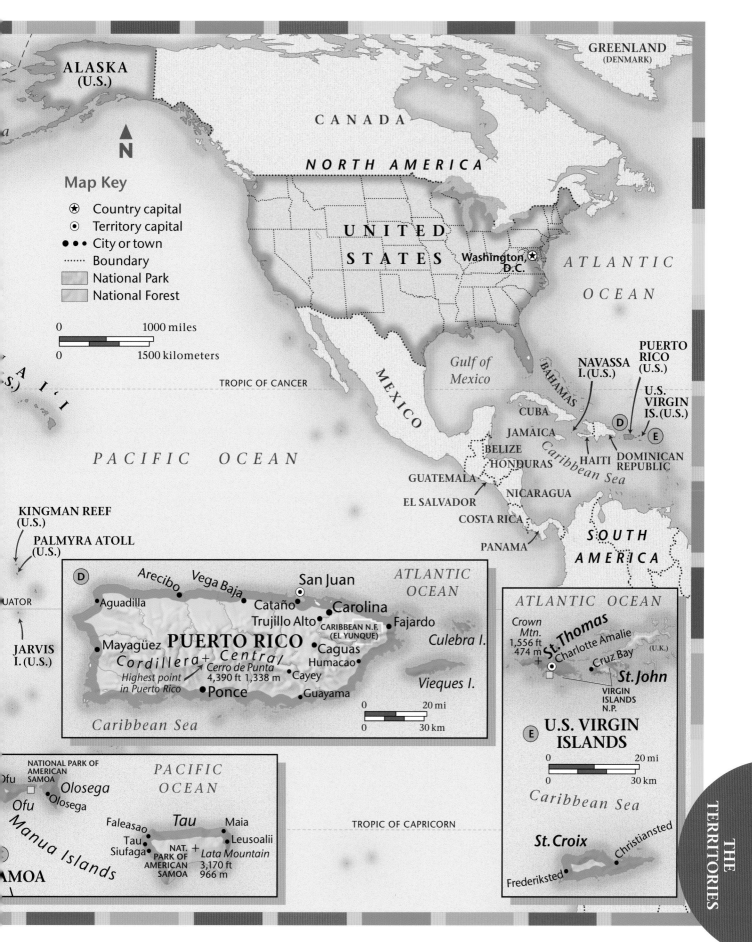

GREENLAND
(DENMARK)

ALASKA
(U.S.)

N

CANADA

NORTH AMERICA

Map Key

⊛ Country capital
⊙ Territory capital
● ● City or town
⋯⋯ Boundary
National Park
National Forest

UNITED
STATES

Washington, ⊛
D.C.

ATLANTIC

OCEAN

0   1000 miles
0   1500 kilometers

TROPIC OF CANCER

Gulf of
Mexico

MEXICO

BAHAMAS

PUERTO
RICO
(U.S.)

NAVASSA
I.(U.S.)

U.S.
VIRGIN
IS.(U.S.)

CUBA

JAMAICA

BELIZE

GUATEMALA

EL SALVADOR

HAITI

Ⓓ

Ⓔ

DOMINICAN
REPUBLIC

*Caribbean
Sea*

PACIFIC   OCEAN

HONDURAS

NICARAGUA

COSTA RICA

PANAMA

SOUTH
AMERICA

KINGMAN REEF
(U.S.)

PALMYRA ATOLL
(U.S.)

UATOR

JARVIS
I.(U.S.)

Ⓓ

Arecibo

Vega Baja

San Juan

*ATLANTIC
OCEAN*

●Aguadilla

Cataño

Carolina

Trujillo Alto

PUERTO RICO

Mayagüez

Cordillera *Central*
Cerro de Punta
Highest point 4,390 ft 1,338 m
in Puerto Rico

Caguas

Humacao●

Cayey

●Ponce

Guayama

CARIBBEAN N.F.
(EL YUNQUE)

Fajardo

Culebra I.

Vieques I.

0   20 mi
0   30 km

Caribbean Sea

ATLANTIC OCEAN

Crown
Mtn.
1,556 ft
474 m

St. Thomas

Charlotte Amalie

(U.K.)

Cruz Bay

⊙

St. John

VIRGIN
ISLANDS
N.P.

Ⓔ **U.S. VIRGIN
ISLANDS**

0   20 mi
0   30 km

Caribbean Sea

NATIONAL PARK OF
AMERICAN
SAMOA

*PACIFIC
OCEAN*

Ofu

Olosega

Olosega

Ofu

Tau

Faleasao   Maia

Tau   ●Leusoalii

Siufaga   NAT. *Lata Mountain*
PARK OF 3,170 ft
AMERICAN 966 m
SAMOA

Manua Islands

TROPIC OF CAPRICORN

AMOA

St. Croix

Christiansted

Frederiksted●

St. Croix

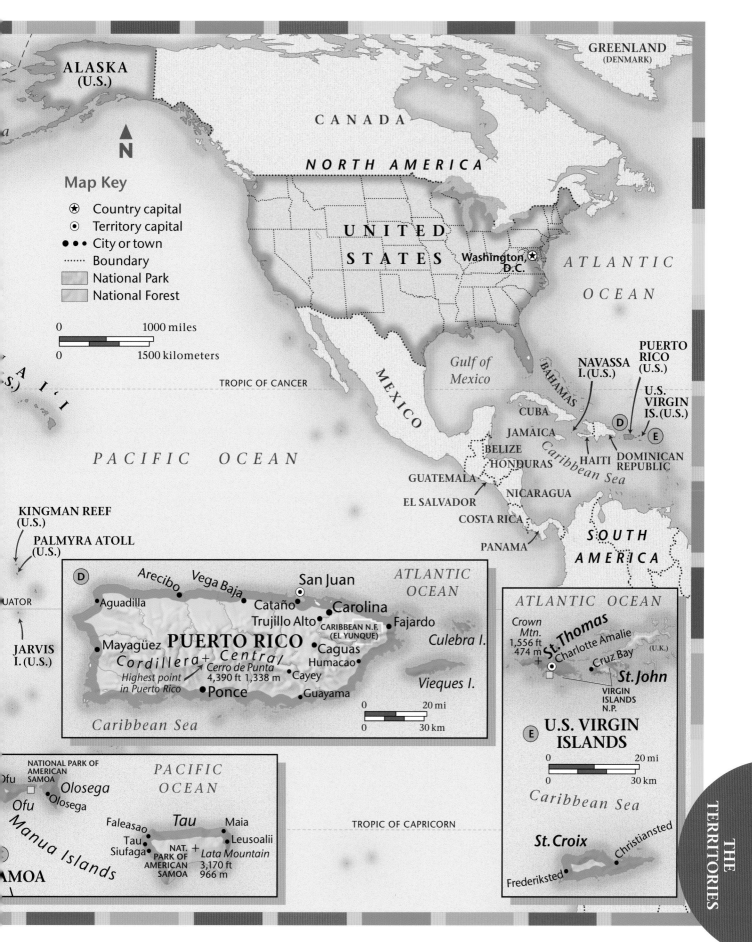

The United States at a Glance

Land
Five Largest States by Area

1. **Alaska:** 663,267 sq mi (1,717,854 sq km)
2. **Texas:** 268,581 sq mi (695,621 sq km)
3. **California:** 163,696 sq mi (423,970 sq km)
4. **Montana:** 147,042 sq mi (380,838 sq km)
5. **New Mexico:** 121,590 sq mi (314,915 sq km)

Water
Primary Water Bodies Bordering the U.S.

1. **Pacific Ocean:** 65,436,200 sq mi (169,479,000 sq km)
2. **Atlantic Ocean:** 35,338,500 sq mi (91,526,400 sq km)
3. **Arctic Ocean:** 5,390,000 sq mi (13,960,100 sq km)
4. **Gulf of Mexico:** 591,430 sq mi (1,531,810 sq km)

Highest, Longest, Largest

The numbers below show locations on the map.

❶ **Highest Mountain**
Mount McKinley (Denali), in Alaska:
20,320 ft (6,194 m)

❷ **Longest River System**
Mississippi–Missouri: 3,710 mi (5,971 km)

❸ **Largest Freshwater Lake**
Lake Superior:
31,700 sq mi (82,103 sq km)

❹ **Largest Saltwater Lake**
Great Salt Lake, in Utah:
1,700 sq mi (4,403 sq km)

❺ **Northern most point**
Point Barrow, Alaska

❻ **Southern most point**
Kalae, Hawai'i

❼ **Eastern most point**
Sail Rock, West Quoddy Head, Maine

❽ **Western most point**
Peaked Island,
Attu Island, Alaska

People

More than 300 million people live in the United States, with about 53 percent of the population living in coastal regions. If the entire population of the U.S. were to stand shoulder to shoulder, everyone would fit into about 44 square miles, an area smaller than the size of Washington, D.C.

Five Largest States by Number of People

1. **California:** 36,756,666 people
2. **Texas:** 24,326,974 people
3. **New York:** 19,490,297 people
4. **Florida:** 18,328,340 people
5. **Illinois:** 12,901,563 people

Five Largest Cities* by Number of People

1. **New York City, NY:** 8,274,527 people
2. **Los Angeles, CA:** 3,834,340 people
3. **Chicago, IL:** 2,836,658 people
4. **Houston, TX:** 2,208,180 people
5. **Phoenix, AZ:** 1,552,259 people

*Figures are for city proper, not metropolitan area.

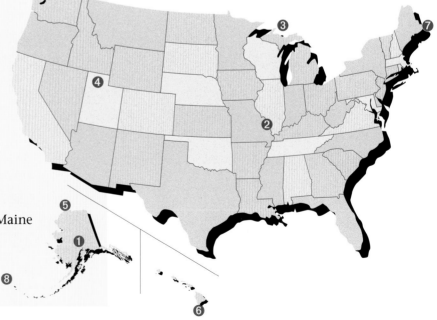

Glossary

Barrier Island: a long sandy island that runs parallel to a shore

Bicentennial: the two-hundredth anniversary of an event

Big Ten Conference: a group of colleges and universities, mostly in the Midwest, known for their sports and academic achievements

Boundary: an imaginary line that separates one political or mapped area from another; physical features, such as mountains and rivers, or latitude and longitude lines sometimes act as boundaries

Capital: a place where a country or state government is located

Coniferous forest: evergreen, needleleaf trees that bear seeds in cones

Container ships: large ships that carry goods in truck-sized metal containers among ports around the world

Continental Divide: a natural boundary line that separates the waters that flow into the Atlantic Ocean and Gulf of Mexico from the waters that flow into the Pacific Ocean

Deciduous forests: species of trees, including oak, maple, and beech, all of which lose their leaves in the cold season

Desert: a region with either hot or cold temperatures that receives 10 inches (25 cm) or less of precipitation a year

Earthquake: shaking and vibration of the earth caused by underground movement

Erosion: the process of wearing away Earth's surface by wind, water, or ice

Estuary: the wide part of a river near a sea, where freshwater and saltwater mix

Exports: products made in one place and sent to another to be sold

Foothills: a region of lower hills at the base of a mountain

Freshwater lakes: bodies of water that are surrounded by land and are not salty

Governor: the head of a state government

Grassland: large areas of mainly flat land covered with grasses

Hydroelectric plant: a facility that uses the motion of water to create power

Ice cap: an area of ice and snow that permanently covers a large area of land

Indian Reservation/I.R.: an area of land set aside by the U.S. government for Native Americans to live on and govern

Livestock: tame animals like cows and horses raised for profit

Pedestrians: people who travel on foot

Peninsula: a large piece of land that sticks out into the water

Petroleum: an energy resource that occurs naturally underground

Powwow: a council or meeting of Native Americans

Rain forest: a region occurring mostly in a belt between the Tropic of Cancer and the Tropic of Capricorn in areas that have at least 80 inches (200 cm) of rain each year and an average yearly temperature of 77°F (25°C)

Seaport: a place where seagoing ships can dock

Sedimentary: a kind of rock made of compressed small particles

Shakers: members of a religious group who did not marry and lived in communal societies

Skyline: the outline of buildings and objects in a city seen against the sky

Territory: land under the rule of a country but that is not a state or a province of that country

Thoroughbred: a breed of horse known for its speed in horse racing; a cross between Arabian stallions and English mares

Totem poles: a post with carvings and paintings that represent family histories; found especially among native peoples of the Pacific Northwest region

Tundra: a region at high latitudes or high elevations that has cold temperatures, low vegetation, and a short growing season

UFO (short for unidentified flying object): An object seen in the sky that some people believe may be flown by beings from outer space

Wetland: land that is either covered with or soaked by water; includes swamps, marshes, and bogs

Index

Pictures and the text that describes them have their page numbers printed in **bold** type.

Two-Letter Postal Codes

ALABAMA	AL
ALASKA	AK
ARIZONA	AZ
ARKANSAS	AR
CALIFORNIA	CA
COLORADO	CO
CONNECTICUT	CT
DELAWARE	DE
DISTRICT OF COLUMBIA	DC
FLORIDA	FL
GEORGIA	GA
HAWAI'I	HI
IDAHO	ID
ILLINOIS	IL
INDIANA	IN
IOWA	IA
KANSAS	KS
KENTUCKY	KY
LOUISIANA	LA
MAINE	ME
MARYLAND	MD
MASSACHUSETTS	MA
MICHIGAN	MI
MINNESOTA	MN
MISSISSIPPI	MS
MISSOURI	MO
MONTANA	MT
NEBRASKA	NE
NEVADA	NV
NEW HAMPSHIRE	NH
NEW JERSEY	NJ
NEW MEXICO	NM
NEW YORK	NY
NORTH CAROLINA	NC
NORTH DAKOTA	ND
OHIO	OH
OKLAHOMA	OK
OREGON	OR
PENNSYLVANIA	PA
PUERTO RICO	PR
RHODE ISLAND	RI
SOUTH CAROLINA	SC
SOUTH DAKOTA	SD
TENNESSEE	TN
TEXAS	TX
UTAH	UT
VERMONT	VT
VIRGINIA	VA
WASHINGTON	WA
WEST VIRGINIA	WV
WISCONSIN	WI
WYOMING	WY

Published by the National Geographic Society

John M. Fahey, Jr.
President and Chief Executive Officer

Gilbert M. Grosvenor
Chairman of the Board

Tim T. Kelly
President, Global Media Group

John Q. Griffin
President, Publishing

Nina D. Hoffman
Executive Vice President; President, Book Publishing Group

Melina Gerosa Bellows
Executive Vice President, Children's Publishing

Prepared by the Book Division

Nancy Laties Feresten
Vice President, Editor in Chief, Children's Books

Bea Jackson
Director of Design and Illustrations, Children's Books

Jennifer Emmett
Executive Editor, Reference and Solo, Children's Books

Amy Shields
Executive Editor, Series, Children's Books

Carl Mehler
Director of Maps

R. Gary Colbert
Production Director

Jennifer A. Thornton
Managing Editor

Staff for this Book

Priyanka Lamichhane
Project Editor

Bea Jackson
Art Director

Lori Renda
Illustrations Editor

Ruthie Thompson
Designer

Michael McNey, Sven M. Dolling
Map Research and Production

Martha Sharma
Writer and Chief Consultant

Erica Rose
Copy Editor

Connie Binder
Indexer

Kathryn Murphy
Editorial Intern

Grace Hill
Associate Managing Editor

Heidi Vincent
Vice President, Direct Response Sales and Marketing

Jeff Reynolds
Marketing Director, Children's Books

Lewis R. Bassford
Production Manager

Susan Borke
Legal and Business Affairs

Manufacturing and Quality Management

Christopher A. Liedel
Chief Financial Officer

Phillip L. Schlosser
Vice President

Chris Brown
Technical Director

Nicole Elliott, Rachel Faulise
Managers

Founded in 1888, the National Geographic Society is one of the largest nonprofit scientific and educational organizations in the world. It reaches more than 285 million people worldwide each month through its official journal, NATIONAL GEOGRAPHIC, and its four other magazines; the National Geographic Channel; television documentaries; radio programs; films; books; videos and DVDs; maps; and interactive media. National Geographic has funded more than 8,000 scientific research projects and supports an education program combating geographic illiteracy.

For more information, please call 1-800-NGS LINE (647-5463) or write to the following address:

NATIONAL GEOGRAPHIC SOCIETY
1145 17th Street NW, Washington, D.C. 20036-4688 U.S.A.

Visit us online at www.nationalgeographic.com/books

ISBN 978-1-4263-0512-2 (trade); 978-1-4263-0558-0 (reinforced library binding)

Illustrations Credits

Abbreviations for terms appearing below: (t)top; (b)-bottom; (l)-left; (r)-right; (c)-center; AL = Alamy; CO = Corbis; GI = Getty Images; IS= iStockPhoto; NGS = NationalGeographicStock.com; PD = PhotoDisc; SS= Shutterstock

Art for state flowers and state birds by Robert E. Hynes

Front cover, Steve Niedorf Photography/The Image Bank/Getty Images

Back cover, (tl), Taylor S. Kennedy/NGS; (tr), italianestro/SS; (br), Glenn Taylor/IS; (bl), Michael Nichols/NGS

Spine, Glenn Taylor/IS

Front of the Book
2 (l), Alaska Stock Images/NGS; 2 (tr), SergeyIT/SS; 2 (br), metalstock/SS; 3 (tl), Zuzule/SS; 3 (tr), Eric Isselée/SS; 3 (cl), James M Phelps, Jr/SS; 3 (cr), Geoffrey Kuchera/SS; 3 (bl), 88 (l), Zuzule/SS; 6 (l), erllre74/SS; 6 (tr), Charles Krebs/Riser/GI; 6 (cr), Mike Brake/SS; 6 (br), James Randklev/Riser/GI; 7, Olivier Le Queinec/SS; 8 (t), Billy Hustace/Stone/GI; 8 (b), Sonya Etchison/SS; 9 (l), Mark R/SS; 9 (r), Pete Seaward/Stone/GI; 10 (l), PD; 10–11, PD; 11 (tr), Taylor S. Kennedy/NGS; 11 (b), Adam Woolfitt/CO

The Northeast
12 (l), Alaska Stock Images/NGS; 12–13, Skip Brown/NGS; 14 up, Shawn Pecor/SS; 14 (b), Donald Gargano/SS; 15, Joel Sartore/NGS; 16 (t), Jake Rajs/Stone/GI; 16 (c), Kevin Fleming/CO; 16 (b), William S. Kuta/AL; 17, Catherine Lane/IS; 18 (t), PD; 18 (c), Mikael Damkier/SS; 18 (b), Jeff Schultes/SS; 19, Noah Strycker/SS; 20 (t), Emory Kristof/NGS; 20 (b), Jeremy Edwards/IS; 21 (t), Justine Gecewicz/IS; 21 (b), James L. Stanfield/NGS; 22 (t), Christopher Penler/SS; 22 (b), Lijuan Guo/SS; 23 (l), Chee-Onn Leong/SS; 23 (r), Brett Atkins/SS; 24 (t), Paula Stephens/SS; 24 (c), Marcel Jancovic/SS; 24 (b), Thomas & Amelia Takacs/SS; 25, Tony Campbell/SS; 26 (t), Dave Raboin/IS; 26 (c), Steve Miller/The Star-Ledger/CO; 26 (b), Aimin Tang/IS; 27 (t), Sheldon Kralstein/IS; 27 (b), Andrew F. Kazmierski/SS; 28 (t), Cathleen Abers-Kimball/IS; 28 (b), Richard Levine/AL; 29, Glenn Taylor/IS; 30, IS; 31 (l), Jeremy Edwards/IS; 31 (r), Racheal Grazias/SS; 32 (t), Yare Marketing/SS; 32 (c), Mona Makela/SS; 32 (b), Joy Brown/SS; 33, Robert Kelsey/SS; 34 (t), Thomas M Perkins/SS; 34 (b), Glenda M. Powers/SS; 35 (t), Parker Deen/IS; 35 (b), rebvt/SS

The Southeast
36 (l), SergeyIT/SS; 36–37, Maria Stenzel/NGS; 38 (t), Darryl Vest/SS; 38 (c), Kevin Fleming/CO; 38 (b), Wayne James/SS; 39, Ronnie Howard/SS; 40 (t), Jaimie Duplass/SS; 40 (b), Bill Barksdale/CO; 41, Travel Bug/SS; 42 (t), Wayne Johnson/IS; 42 (b), Alan Freed/SS; 43 (t), Varina and Jay Patel/IS; 43 (b), Valentyn Volkov/SS; 44 (t), jackweichen_gatech/SS; 44 (c), Antonio V. Oquias/SS; 44 (b), Michael Carlucci/IS; 45, Andrew F. Kazmierski/SS; 46 (t), Leon Ritter/SS; 46 (c), Craig Wactor/SS; 46 (b), Anne Kitzman/SS; 47, Neale Cousland/SS; 48 (t), Bob Sacha/CO; 48 (c), Jim Richardson/CO; 48 (b), J. Helgason/SS; 49 (l), Stephen Helstowski/SS; 49 (r), Kathryn Bell/SS; 50 (t), Vilmos Varga/SS; 50 (c), Chad Purser/IS; 50 (b), Peter Arnold, Inc./AL; 51, Mike Flippo/SS; 52 (l), Leah-Anne Thompson/SS; 52 (r), Forrest L. Smith, III/SS; 53 (l), Rob Byron/SS; 53 (r), Brad Whitsitt/SS; 54, Rafael Ramirez Lee/SS; 55 (t), Denise Kappa/SS; 55 (b), Zach Holmes/AL; 56 (t), Envision/CO; 56 (b), Bryan Busovicki/SS; 57 (l), Wayne James/SS; 57 (r), Jennifer King/SS; 58 (t), Darren K. Fisher/SS; 58 (b), Travel Bug/SS; 59 (l), graham s. klotz/SS; 59 (r), Adam Bies/SS; 60 (t), Robert Pernell/SS; 60 (c), Ken Inness/SS; 60 (t), Mary Terriberry/SS; 61, Adam Bies/SS

The Midwest
62 (l), metalstock/SS; 62–63, Jim Richardson/NGS; 64 (t), Ralf-Finn Hestoft/CO; 64 (c), Tim Boyle/GI; 64 (t), Jenny Solomon/SS; 65, Kim Karpeles/AL; 66 (t), James Steidl/SS; 66 (b), Todd Taulman/SS; 66 (c), John J Klaiber Jr./SS; 66 (b), Melissa Farlow/NGS; 68 (t), jokter/SS; 68 (b), Madeleine Openshaw/SS; 69 (l), Steve Schneider/IS; 69 (r), Andre Jenny/AL; 70 (t), aceshot1/SS; 70 (b), Rusty Dodson/SS; 71, Bruce Dale/NGS; 72 (t), Gary Paul Lewis/SS; 72 (c), Rachel L. Sellers/SS; 72 (b), The Final Image/SS; 73, Cornelia Schaible/SS; 74 (t), Maxim Kulko/SS; 74 (c), V. J. Matthew/SS; 74 (b), Geoffrey Kuchera/SS; 75, Karla Caspari/SS; 76 (t), Neil Phillip Mey/SS; 76 (b), Jose Gil/SS; 77 (l), Tim Pleasant/SS; 77 (r), Rusty Dodson/SS; 78 (t), Bates Littlehales/NGS; 78 (b), James L. Amos/NGS; 79 (t), Joel Sartore/NGS; 79 (b), Jim Richardson/NGS; 80 (t), Ian Martin/NGS; 80 (c), Randy Olson/NGS; 80 (b), Rusty Dodson/SS; 81, iofoto/SS; 82 (t), aceshot1/SS; 82 (c), Alex Neauville/SS; 82 (b), James M Phelps, Jr/SS; 83, Rena Schild/SS; 84 (t), Werner Bollmann/Photolibrary/GI; 84 (c), Ira Block/NGS; 84 (b), iofoto/SS; 85, Danita Delimont/AL; 86 (tl), Aga/SS; 86 (tr), Brad Thompson/SS; 86 (c), Volkman K. Wentzel/NGS; 86 (b), Alvis Upitis/AgStock Images/CO; 87, Layne Kennedy/CO

The Southwest
88 (l), Zuzule/SS; 88–89, Jack Dykinga/NGS; 90 (t), Michael Nichols/NGS; 90 (c), Zschnepf/SS; 90 (b), Chris Curtis/SS; 92 (t), italianestro/SS; 92 (c), Mariusz S. Jurgielewicz/SS; 92 (b), Ralph Lee Hopkins/NGS; 94 (t), Clint Spencer/IS; 94 (b), Phil Anthony/SS; 95 (l), Lindsay Hebberd/CO; 95 (r), MWaits/SS; 96 (t), Ben Conlan/IS; 96 (c), Mira/AL; 96 (b), Rusty Dodson/SS; 97, B. Anthony Stewart/NGS

The West
98 (l), Eric Isselée/SS; 98–99, Gordon Wiltsie/NGS; 100 (t), Benoit Rousseau/IS; 100 (b), Alysta/SS; 101, Michael Pemberton/SS; 102 (t), Stas Volik/SS; 102 (c), Bates Littlehales/NGS; 102 (b), Lindsay Noechel/SS; 103, Elke Dennis/SS; 104 (t), Larsek/SS; 104 (b), PD; 105, John Kelly/Iconica/GI; 106 (t), Jarvis Gray/SS; 106 (c), Jim Sugar/CO; 106 (b), Alex Staroseltsev/SS; 107 (t), Steve Raymer/NGS; 107 (b), Jeff Hunter/Photographer's Choice/GI; 108 (t), Bryan Brazil/SS; 108 (c), Raymond Gehman/NGS; 108 (b), David P. Smith/SS; 109, Dick Durrance II/NGS; 110 (t), Noah Clayton/The Image Bank/GI; 110 (b), Doug Lemke/SS; 111 (l), Geoffrey Kuchera/SS; 111 (r), Jerry Sharp/SS; 112 (t), Andy Z./SS; 112 (c), W. Robert Moore/NGS; 112 (b), Sam Abell/NGS; 113, Danita Delimont/AL; 114 (t), Jennifer Lynn Arnold/SS; 114 (c), Rachell Coe/SS; 114–115, Peter Kunasz/SS; 115 (r), Tischenko Irina/SS; 116 (t), Grafton Marshall Smith/CO; 116 (c), Nelson Sirlin/SS; 116 (b), PD; 118 (t), Natalia Bratslavsky/SS; 118 (b), Luis Salazar/SS; 119 (l), Oksana Perkins/SS; 119 (r), Sandy Buckley/SS; 120 (t), Videowokart/SS; 120 (b), Henryk Sadura/SS; 121 (l), Peter Kunasz/SS; 121 (r), Michael Rubin/SS

For information about special discounts for bulk purchases, please contact National Geographic Books Special Sales: ngspecsales@ngs.org

For rights or permissions inquires, please contact National Geographic Books Subsidiary Rights: ngbookrights@ngs.org

Printed in China
14/PPS/3

RUSSIA

ARCTIC OCEAN

60° N

180°

160° W

140° W

THE WEST
pages 98–121

160° E

40° N

PACIFIC OCEAN

0   600 miles

0   900 kilometers

Albers Conic Equal-Area Projection

180°

20° N

THE WEST
pages 98–121

160° W

140° W